REVELATION
Brought Down To Earth

FRANK BIELA

REVELATION Brought Down to Earth
by Frank Biela
ISBN: 978-1-935018-72-8
Copyright © 2014 by Frank Biela
Revised edition
All rights reserved by Frank Biela
For permission to republish or reprint any portion of this book please email the author at:
Revelation21st@gmail.com
Interior Design: Leo Ward
Cover Design: Joe Zgoda
Edited by: Louise Biela

Published by:
5 Stones Publishing
A division of The International Localization Network, Inc.

Bibles used:
1. New King James Version (Prophecy Study Bible, John C. Hagee); Thomas Nelson Inc.; copyright 1997. Scriptures taken from the New King James Version. Copyright 1979, 1980, 1982 by Thomas Nelson, Inc. Used by permission. All rights reserved.
2. Scripture taken from the Holy Bible, New International Version. Copyright 1973, 1978, 1984 by International Bible Society. Used by permission of International Bible Society.
3. King James Version (reference edition); Thomas Nelson Inc.; copyright 1972.

Books used:
1. Dispensational Truth; by Clarence Larkin; copyright 1918; enlarged and revised edition copyrighted 1920
2. The Book of Revelation; by Clarence Larkin; copyright 1919
3. The New Strong's Exhaustive Concordance of the Bible; copyright 1984
4. Harper's Bible Dictionary; copyright 1985

DEDICATION

I dedicate this book to my Lord and Savior Jesus Christ. I thank you Lord with all my heart and soul.

To my wife Louise who without her love, encouragement, support and prayer I might have given up. Her determination to never give up was a true inspiration for me to finish this book. Her suggestions and ideas were invaluable. I love you with all my heart and soul!

Frank

TABLE OF CONTENTS

DEDICATION 3
CHAPTER 1 7
CHAPTER 2 21
CHAPTER 3 37
CHAPTER 4 55
CHAPTER 5 61
CHAPTER 6 67
CHAPTER 7 79
CHAPTER 8 85
CHAPTER 9 91
CHAPTER 10 99
CHAPTER 11 103
CHAPTER 12 115
CHAPTER 13 127
CHAPTER 14 149
CHAPTER 15 163
CHAPTER 16 169
CHAPTER 17 181
CHAPTER 18 201
CHAPTER 19 209
CHAPTER 20 221
CHAPTER 21 231
CHAPTER 22 243
About the Author 253

CHAPTER 1

Revelation 1:1

> *"The Revelation of Jesus Christ, which God gave Him, to show His servants things which must shortly take place. And He sent and signified it by His angel to His servant John,"*

As the Book of Revelation begins, the first verse reveals this book is "The Revelation of Jesus Christ" not the revelation of the apostle John. Christ's own Father (God) gave this revelation to Him to show His followers things that must shortly come to pass. Jesus leaves no room for doubt that the things in this book will happen. There is nothing that can stop or change these things from happening just as all other scriptures up to the present time have been fulfilled to the very *"jot and tittle" (Matthew 5:18)*. Some prophecies in scripture were written hundreds, and some thousands of years before they happened yet they were and still are being fulfilled exactly as scripture said they would be.

John tells us it is an angel sent by Jesus who presents this revelation to him so he could pass it on to the rest of the world.

Revelation 1:2

> *"Who bore witness to the word of God, and to the testimony of Jesus Christ, and to all things that he saw."*

John was a true witness to God's word because Jesus was his friend and companion. John shared in Christ's life as he talked, ate and walked with Jesus.

Revelation 1:3

> *"Blessed is he who reads and those who hear the words of this prophecy, and keep those things which are written in it; for the time is near."*

The word "blessed" in the Greek language is *"makarios"* which means supremely blessed, fortunate, well off.

If you cannot read this book yourself, have someone read it to you so you hear the word and receive a blessing. Ask God to open your spiritual understanding. Why? *"Because the time is near"* It is close, it is very close.

[SEE ALSO: PROVERBS 8:34; LUKE 11:28; JOHN 8:51; REVELATION 22:7]

Revelation 1:4

> *"John, to the seven churches which are in Asia: Grace to you and peace from Him who is and who was and who is to come, and from the seven Spirits who are before His throne,"*

The seven churches John is writing to are located on the western end of Asia Minor (located on a major mail route, now modern day Turkey, and cover an area about the size of the state of Pennsylvania.) Each one was chosen for certain characteristics typical of Christ's church, not only in John's day, but would remain typical through the centuries until the church is removed from this earth. Some characteristics of these churches were their works, labor, patience, inability to tolerate evil, tribulation, poverty, hate of blasphemy, faithfulness unto death, charity and keepers of God's word.

Some also believe the churches represent seven distinct church periods defined by church history. I believe the scriptures reveal that the seven churches represent all of the above.

John sends a salutation to the seven churches in Asia on behalf of God, and at the same time to God. In verses 4-6, it is unique how John shifts and twists the salutation. He begins with the benediction: *"Grace to you and peace from Him who is, and who was, and who is to come."* At first glance a person might presume that the salutation is from Jesus, but as you look closely it is clearly from the whole Godhead: Father, Son and Holy Spirit.

[SEE ALSO: JOHN 14:9A; II CORINTHIANS 4:4; COLOSSIANS 2:9]

"HIM" who is and who was and who is to come;" is speaking of God the Father, because in the next verse it says: *"And from Jesus Christ"*. In *Revelation 1:8* Jesus says: *"I am the Alpha and the Omega, the Beginning and the End, says the Lord, who is, and who was, and who is to come, the Almighty."*

Jesus claims the same title as His Father which shows that Jesus and the Father are one. Scriptures in the Old and New Testament support this claim.

[SEE ALSO: GENESIS 1:26; JOHN 1:1; 10:30; I CORINTHIANS 8:6; COLOSSIANS 1:14&15; I TIMOTHY 3:16]

Revelation 1:4 ends with "And from the seven Spirits (Holy Spirit) which are before His throne;"

The seven Spirits of God mentioned in Isaiah 11:2 are:

> *"The Spirit of the Lord, the Spirit of Wisdom, the Spirit of Understanding, the Spirit of Counsel, the Spirit of Might, the Spirit of Knowledge and the Fear of the Lord."*

[SEE ALSO: FURTHER EXPLANATION OF THE SEVEN SPIRITS IN CHAPTER 5.]

In Scripture numbers are often symbolic. Seven is considered a sacred number which refers to the perfection of God being *all in all*; Father, Son and Holy Spirit.

Revelation 1:5

> *"And from Jesus Christ, the faithful witness, the first born from the dead, and the ruler over the kings of the earth. To Him who loved us and washed us from our sins in His own blood,"*

Jesus has shown His faithfulness through His death and resurrection, therefore, He can be believed and trusted in what He shows John in this book. He sacrificed his own blood and carried it into the heavenly tabernacle thereby performing the work of the High Priest.

[SEE ALSO: JEREMIAH 42:5A; REVELATION 3:14]

Revelation 1:6

> *"And has made us kings and priests to His God and Father, to Him be glory and dominion forever and ever. Amen."*

Jesus will be the King of kings when He takes the throne on earth, and we will be kings and priests ruling and reigning with Him.

Revelation 1:7

> *"Behold, He is coming with clouds, and every eye will see Him, and they also who pierced Him. And all the tribes of the earth will mourn because of Him. Even so, Amen."*

The same way Christ ascended into heaven after His resurrection, so He will return, in the clouds.

> *"And then shall appear the sign of the Son of Man in heaven: and then shall all the tribes of the earth mourn, and they*

> *shall see the Son of Man coming in the clouds of heaven with power and great glory." (Matthew 24:30)*

[SEE ALSO: ACTS 1:9-11]

Whenever God showed Himself in the cloud, the "Glory" of God is mentioned. Jesus is the Glory of God manifested in the image of man.

[SEE ALSO: EXODUS 16:10; II CHRONICLES 5:13C&14; DANIEL 7:13]

When Christ comes back He will usher in the 1,000-year peaceful millennium.

> *"Blessed and holy is he who has part in the first resurrection. Over such the second death has no power, but they shall be priests of God and of Christ, and shall reign with Him a thousand years." (Revelation 20:6)*

The Lord will destroy all the unbelievers and establish Israel in the Promised Land, as promised to their fathers Abraham, Isaac, and Jacob.

The reason *"All the tribes of the earth will mourn"* at Christ's return to the earth instead of rejoicing is because these tribes (nations) are followers of the antichrist, the beast and the false prophet. They did not believe Jesus Christ was God or that He was coming back. Now that they know the Scriptures and God are true, it is too late. These tribes will be destroyed when Christ returns. When the 1,000 year millennium ends they will be judged and sentenced by God at the "White Throne Judgment." They will be told where their place in the Lake of Fire will be along with Satan, the Beast and the False Prophet.

[SEE ALSO: REVELATION 20:10-15]

John closes *Revelation 1:7* with *"Even so, Amen."* What John seems to be saying with these three simple words are "Yeah, it sounds horrible that all those people are going to die and be cast into the Lake of Fire for all eternity, but they had the same chance to know and accept Jesus died for their sins as everybody else. They chose to reject Christ, so they are getting what they justly deserve."

Revelation 1:8

> "I am Alpha and Omega, the beginning and the ending, says the Lord, which is, and which was, and which is to come, the Almighty."

Christ is not saying that He had a beginning and an ending. The Lord is saying: He created the beginning of everything, and He will end everything. Christ Himself always was and always will be, so that when everything else ceases to exist and all ages come to an end, the Lord will still be.

> "IN the beginning was the Word (Jesus), and the Word (Jesus) was with God, and the Word (Jesus) was (is) God. The same was in the beginning with God. All things were made by Him (Jesus); and without Him (Jesus) was not anything made that was made." (John 1:1-3)

When nothing existed in the visible realm, scripture says it was Jesus who made the invisible, visible, which means He had to already exist.

[SEE ALSO: ISAIAH 41:4; ROMANS 1:20; COLOSSIANS 1: 16&17; REVELATION 4:8, 11:16&17]

> "And He said unto me, it is done. I am Alpha and Omega, the Beginning and the End." (Revelation 21:6)

> "I am Alpha and Omega, the Beginning and the End, the First and the Last." (Revelation 22:13)

Jesus could not make these statements if they weren't true since God is truth and incapable of lying.

[SEE ALSO: TITUS 1:2; JOHN 3:33]

Revelation 1:9

> "I, John, both your brother and companion in tribulation, and in the kingdom and patience of Jesus Christ, was on the island that is called Patmos for the word of God and for the testimony of Jesus Christ."

John knew Jesus was God. He was an eye witness to Jesus' miracles. He was there when Jesus died on the cross and he saw Jesus after He rose from the dead. John was not afraid to proclaim the good news of the Gospel.

John was arrested and exiled to the Island of Patmos located on the Aegean Sea off the coast of Greece because of his faith. While in exile the Lord appeared to John and revealed to him this vision and told him to write everything down which John did around 95 A.D.

John calls us his *"brother and companion in tribulation"*. John was known as the apostle Jesus loved, probably his closest friend. Yet he did not escape tribulation and persecution so certainly we will not. Jesus said we would have tribulation in this world even though we are believers.

> "In the world you will have tribulation (troubles): but be of good cheer; I have overcome the world." (John 16:33b)

> Christ also said: "If they have persecuted Me, they will also persecute you; if they have kept My saying, they will keep yours also." (John 15:20b)

John depended on Christ to get him through the trials and tribulations and we need to do the same. The apostle Peter encourages us with these words:

> "Dear friends, do not be surprised at the painful trial you are suffering, as though something strange were happening to you. But rejoice that you participate in the sufferings

of Christ; so that you may be overjoyed when His glory is revealed. If you are insulted because of the name of Christ, you are blessed, for the Spirit of Glory and of God rests on you. If you suffer, it should not be as a murderer, or thief or any other kind of criminal, or even as a meddler. However if you suffer as a Christian, do not be ashamed; but praise God that you bear that name." (1 Peter 4:12-16 NIV)

Revelation 1:10&11

"I was in the Spirit on the Lord's Day, and I heard behind me a loud voice, as of a trumpet, saying, "I am the Alpha and the Omega, the First and the Last," and, "What you see, write in a book and send it to the seven churches which are in Asia: to Ephesus, to Smyrna, to Pergamos, to Thyatira, to Sardis, to Philadelphia, and to Laodicea.""

John was *"in the Spirit"* being one with the Lord on the *"Lord's day"*, (probably in a trance like state). Some people believe this means John's spirit was at the "LORD'S DAY" (the day of vengeance and of the Lord's return to earth to usher in the millennium) but that does not make sense. In verse12 John says he *"turned to see the voice"* indicating he was still *physically* and *spiritually* on the Isle of Patmos at the time the Lord spoke to him. John was simply deep in spiritual meditation on the Sabbath. John goes on to say that the voice he heard behind him was *"a great voice, like of a trumpet."*

Jesus told John to write down everything that He was about to show him and send it on to the seven churches. They represented seven specific church ages which began in 30A.D. through the present 21st century.

Ephesus: An apostate (backslidden) church, from 30A.D. to 100A.D was in danger of "diminishing love".

Smyrna: Persecuted church, from the end of the apostolic church age to Emperor Constantine; 100A.D. to 300 A.D. Its danger was "fear of suffering".

Pergamum: Was a state church that was sexually unrestrained. It existed from Emperor Constantine to Boniface III; 300A.D. to 606A.D. Its danger was "doctrinal compromise".

The above three churches existed during what we know as the *"Ancient History"* period.

Thyatira: Was a Papal church that was very lax in its teachings. It existed from Boniface III to the Reformation; 606A.D. to 1500A.D.

The above period is known as *"Mediaeval History"* or the dark ages.

Sardis: Was a Reformed church which was in danger of becoming spiritually dead. It existed from the reformation to the Peace of Westphalia; 1500A.D. to 1650A.D.

Philadelphia: Was a Missionary church which was a spiritually favored church. It existed from the Peace of Westphalia 1650A.D. to 1900A.D. Its danger was "failing to advance".

Laodicea: Was an Apostate church which was spiritually lukewarm. It existed from 1900A.D. to the present day. Its danger is of "being vomited out of the Lord's mouth".

The above three churches are known as the *"Modern History"* age.

All seven church ages are now present in the 21st century churches. The warnings given to the seven churches are also a warning for today's churches.

Revelation 1:12

"Then I turned to see the voice that spoke with me. And having turned I saw seven golden lampstands,"

At first John was not sure who was talking to him because his back was to the voice. When he turned to see who it was, he saw the seven beautiful golden lampstands which represent the seven churches.

> "The mystery of the seven stars that you saw in My right hand, and of the seven golden lampstands is this: The seven stars are the angels (pastors) of the seven churches: and the seven lampstands are the seven churches" (Revelation 1:20)(NIV).

Revelation 1:13

> "And in the midst of the seven lampstands One like the Son of Man, clothed with a garment down to the feet and girded about the chest with a golden band."

Daniel saw a similar vision of our Lord (DANIEL 7:13&14). The prophet Ezekiel also had a similar vision *(Ezekiel 1:26-28)*.

Revelation 1:14

> "His head and His hair were white like wool, as white as snow, and His eyes like a flame of fire;"

John continues with the description of what he saw. When Daniel 7:9, 13&14 is compared with Revelation 1:14 and Revelation 2:18, there is an amazing, even startling similarity. John describes Jesus in Revelation 1:14&15 looking exactly like Daniel describes God the Father looking in Daniel 7:9. Truly, Jesus and the Father are one, yet two separate Beings.

Revelation 1:15

> "His feet were like fine brass, as if refined in a furnace, and His voice as the sound of many waters;"
>
> John says Christ's feet were *"like fine brass refined in a furnace"*. Jesus walks in absolute truth and justice.

John says Jesus voice was *"like the sound of many waters"*.

> "Behold the glory of the God of Israel (the Father) came from the way of the East: and His voice was like a noise of many waters:" (Ezekiel 43:2)

Again we have the comparison of Old and New Testament showing that the Father and Son are one.

Revelation 1:16

> "He had in His right hand seven stars, out of His mouth went a sharp two-edged sword, and His countenance was like the sun shining in its strength."

Verse 20 reveals that the seven stars represent the *"angels of the seven churches"*. The word "angels" in the Greek is *"aggelos"*, pronounced *(ang-el-os)* and means a messenger by implication, a pastor (to bring tidings). In this verse it means the pastors of the seven churches.

> "For the priest's lips should preserve knowledge, and from his mouth men should seek instruction - for he is the messenger of the Lord Almighty." (Malachi 2:7)(NIV)

Hebrews 4:12 reveals that the two-edged sword represents God's holy word:

> "For the word of God is quick, and powerful, and sharper than any two-edged sword, piercing even to the dividing asunder of soul and spirit, and of the joints and marrow, and is a discerner of the thoughts and intents of the heart."

> "And the sword of the Spirit, which is the word of God." (Ephesians 6:17b)

Revelation 1:17-18

> "And when I saw Him, I fell at His feet as dead. But He laid His right hand on me, saying to me, "Do not be afraid; I am

the First and the Last. I am He who lives, and was dead, and behold, I am alive forevermore. Amen. And I have the keys of Hades and of Death.""

John was awestruck at the presence of Christ standing in front of him in all His glory. So overwhelming was this magnificent sight that John *"fell down at His feet as dead."* In other words; John fainted. Jesus touched him to revive him. To take away John's fear Jesus reassured him that He is the same person that John knew and loved while He walked on this earth. These words must have brought comfort to John as the death and resurrection of Christ is what John had been preaching for over 60 years and the reason he was exiled to the Isle of Patmos.

Christ further comforted John by telling him that it was He (Jesus) who has the keys of Hades and of Death. The only one who could have them is the one who conquered them which means that Hades and Death are real places and He has the power over them.

Revelation 1:19

"Write the things which you have seen, and the things which are, and the things which will take place after this."

This is the revealing of all the Old and New Testament prophesies yet to be fulfilled.

Revelation 1:20

"The mystery of the seven stars which you saw in My right hand, and the seven golden lampstands: The seven stars are the angels of the seven churches, and the seven lampstands which you saw are the seven churches."

The Lord clarifies what the meaning of the stars and lampstands are. The "stars" represent the angels (pastors) of the seven churches *(Revelation1:16)* and the Lord is holding them in His right hand which means no one can harm them unless the Lord allows it. No one is strong enough to take anyone out of God's hand.

> "For I am persuaded, that neither death, nor life, nor angels, nor principalities, nor powers, nor things present, nor things to come, nor height, nor depth, nor any other creature, shall be able to separate us from the love of God, which is in Christ Jesus our Lord." (Romans 8:38&39)

The lampstands represent the seven churches John will be writing letters to.

CHAPTER 2

Church of Ephesus

Revelation 2:1-7a

> "To the angel of the church of Ephesus write, 'These things says He who holds the seven stars in His right hand, who walks in the midst of the seven golden lampstands: I know your works, your labor, your patience, and that you cannot bear those who are evil. And you have tested those who say they are apostles and are not, and have found them liars; and you have persevered and have patience, and have labored for My name's sake and have not become weary. Nevertheless I have this against you, that you have left your first love. Remember therefore from where you have fallen; repent and do the first works, or else I will come to you quickly and remove your lampstand from its place- unless you repent. But this you have, that you hate the deeds of the Nicolaitans, which I also hate. He who has an ear, let him hear what the Spirit says to the churches."

Ephesus was an urban center in the Roman Empire made up of the rich and poor, cultured and ignorant. It was a gathering place of false religious cults and superstitions. A port city of western Asia Minor at the mouth of the Cayster River which lies between Smyrna and Miletus, it is located in what is modern day Turkey. Ephesus was once known as "The Market of Asia." During the time of the apostles Ephesus was the wealthiest and greatest city in all of Asia because it was easily accessible by land and highways connected it to all the major cities North, South and East of it.

The "Temple of Artemis", built for the goddess Diana was one of seven ancient wonders of the world located in Ephesus. Ephesus was over forty years old when Christ told John to write this message and send it to them.

John writes to the pastors of the churches that Jesus is watching what they are doing and how they are behaving. Christ reassures the pastors of the churches that He is holding them in His right hand and taking care of them.

In Revelation 2:2&3 Christ praises the churches, but Paul, who founded the church of Ephesus, warned what might happen to them if they take their focus off Jesus Christ (Acts 20:29&30). Even though the Ephesus church did mighty works, labored hard and did not put up with false teachings or false apostles, church men arose speaking perverse things to draw away disciples just as Paul warned. They were known as the "Nicolaitanes". This was not a sect or religion, but a party within the church who were trying to establish a priestly order. They led a life of self-indulgence and immorality. They were denounced for eating food sacrificed to idols and for practicing sexual perverseness within the church.

The word Nicolaitanes comes from two Greek words: *Nikao* - to conquer, and *Laos*- the people. From this party "to conquer the people" started the whole practice of clergy ruling over the people (laity) which was totally foreign to the New Testament plan. Instead of pastors, deacons and bishops establishing churches, there were now archbishops, cardinals and popes ruling over the people. Christ compliments the Ephesians for standing against this and hating it, just as Christ said He hates it.

[SEE ALSO: PROVERBS 6:16; ECCLESIASTES 3:8; ISAIAH 61:8; MALACHI 1:2&3; ROMANS 9:13; REVELATION 2:15]

Eventually the church at Ephesus got caught up in works and put works ahead of Jesus, making them more important than worshipping the Savior.

A person does not get to heaven by works nor can they earn their way there by works.

> *"For it is by grace you have been saved, through faith - and this not from yourselves, it is the gift of God - Not by works, so that no one can boast. For we are God's workmanship, created in Christ Jesus to do good works, which God prepared in advance for us to do." (Ephesians 2:8-10)*

[SEE ALSO: TITUS 3:8; JAMES 2:17-22, 26]

Jesus warned the Ephesus church if they did not repent He *"Would come quickly, and will remove their candlestick (church) out of its place"*. Ephesus did not repent and the history of the Ephesus church only lasted from 33A.D. to 100A.D. and by 252A.D. not only was the Ephesus church destroyed, but the entire City of Ephesus was destroyed as well. The word Ephesus means to "let go", or to "relax".

Revelation 2:7b

> *"To him who overcomes I will give to eat from the tree of life, which is in the midst of the paradise of God."*

This verse confirms that the "Garden of Eden" and the "Tree of Life" were real and still exist today *(Revelation 22:2)* and that *Paradise* and the *Garden of Eden* are one and the same place.

> *"The tree of life also in the midst of the garden," (Genesis 2:9)*

> *"The tree of life, which is in the midst of the paradise of God," (Revelation 2:7)*

Church of Smyrna

Revelation 2:8-11

> *"And to the angel of the church of Smyrna write, "These things say the First and the Last, who was dead, and came to life: I know your works, tribulation, and poverty (but you are rich); and I know the blasphemy of those who say they are Jews and are not, but are a synagogue of Satan. Do not fear any of those things which you are about to suffer. Indeed, the devil is about to throw some of you into prison, that you may be tested, and you will have tribulation ten days. Be faithful until death, and I will give you the crown of life. He who has an ear, let him hear what the Spirit says to the churches. He who overcomes shall not be hurt by the second death."*

Smyrna today is known as Izmir located in Turkey. It was considered the proudest and most beautiful city in Asia. Historians believe it was the most exquisite city the Greeks ever built, located about 35 miles north of Ephesus and considered by Rome to be its loyal ally. Known as the center for emperor worship under Emperor Domitian, emperor worship was mandatory for every Roman citizen on threat of death.

Smyrna's root meaning is "bitterness", and "myrrh", an ointment associated with death because it was used in preparing bodies for burial.

In His message to this church, the Lord again mentions His people's works but instead of elaborating on the works (as He did with the Ephesians' church), He says: *"I know your works, tribulation and poverty."* The believers lost their means of livelihood as a result of their conversion to Christianity and their refusal to worship the emperor as a god. By making a public confession of their faith it meant poverty, hunger, imprisonment and most of the time, death. Followers of Jesus were thrown to the lions, burned at the stake, or crucified.

Revelation 2:8b

> "These things say the First and the Last, who was dead, and came to life:"

This statement is supported throughout scripture:

> "Do not be afraid; I am the First and the Last. I am He who lives, and was dead, and behold, I am alive forevermore. Amen." (Revelation 1:17b&18)

> "I am the First, and I am the Last; and beside Me there is no God." (Isaiah 44:6)

[SEE ALSO: REVELATION 1:8&11; 22:13; ISAIAH 41:4; 48:12]

Revelation 2:9

> "I know your works, tribulation, and poverty (but you are rich); and I know the blasphemy of those who say they are Jews and are not, but are a synagogue of Satan."

Christ reaffirms the church that even though they are physically poor and in tribulation, they are spiritually rich.

[SEE ALSO: I CORINTHIANS 3:21-23; II CORINTHIANS 6:10; REVELATION 3:17&18]

Every word the Lord speaks to this suffering church is one of appreciation.

Only two of the seven churches, Smyrna and Philadelphia received letters of total commendation and encouragement.

The churches were persecuted because they refused to bow down to Caesar which was mandatory by the time the Book of Revelation was written around 95A.D. or 96A.D.

The Jews mentioned are those who turned the Christians over to the Roman emperor for not worshipping Caesar and burning incense to him claiming *Caesar is lord*.

Polycarp was the pastor of the Smyrna church and was a student and disciple of the apostle John. Polycarp's ministry ended in 156A.D. when persecution of Christians increased. Many women had to stand and watch as their children were tortured, raped, ripped apart, and/or burned alive before they themselves were killed.

Polycarp was burned at the stake at the age of 91. When Polycarp was about to be burned at the stake, he was asked one more time if he would worship Caesar as lord. Polycarp replied that for 86 years he worshipped Christ as Lord and was never disappointed or persecuted by God so why would he change now. The emperor told Polycarp he will burn at the stake for this. Polycarp replied back: *"I will burn at the stake, and within one hour my body will be consumed, but you will burn forever in the fires of hell."* With that, Polycarp was burned at the stake, and as the fire leapt around him, he thanked God that the Lord found him worthy to die as a martyr for Christ.

Revelation 2:10

> *"Do not fear any of those things which you are about to suffer. Indeed, the devil is about to throw some of you into prison, that you may be tested, and you will have tribulation ten days. Be faithful until death, and I will give you the crown of life."*

The author of their suffering was Satan. Satan works through human agents, but it is he who is the ultimate source of persecution. The duration *"ten days"* may be a prophetic reference to the ten

great persecutions under the Roman emperors, beginning with Nero in 64A.D, and ending with Diocletian in 310A.D. Seven of these great persecutions happened during the Smyrna period of church history. It may also refer to the ten years of the last and fiercest persecution under Emperor Diocletian. It could have meant a literal ten days, or, it could have meant all the above.
[SEE ALSO: MATTHEW 24:13]

To those who refuse to worship false idols and not put anything above the Lord, Christ promises a *"crown of life"*.

> *"Blessed is the man who perseveres under trial, because when he has stood the test, he will receive the crown of life that God has promised to those who love Him." (James 1:12)*

Revelation 2:11b

> *"He who overcomes shall not be hurt by the second death."*

The second death is known as the *"White Throne Judgment"* spoken of in Revelation 20:11-15.
[SEE ALSO: MATTHEW 10:28-33]

These are promises from the Lord that were meant not just for the church in Smyrna, but for the church through all the ages right into the 21st century.

CHURCH OF PERGAMOS

Revelation 2:12-17

> *"And to the angel of the church in Pergamos write, "These things says He who has the sharp two-edged sword: I know your works, and where you dwell, where Satan's throne is. And you hold fast to My name, and did not deny My faith even in the days in which Antipas was My faithful martyr,*

who was killed among you, where Satan dwells. But I have a few things against you, because you have there those who hold the doctrine of Balaam, who taught Balak to put a stumbling block before the children of Israel, to eat things sacrificed to idols, and to commit sexual immorality. Thus you also have those who hold the doctrine of the Nicolaitans, which thing I hate. Repent; or else I will come to you quickly and will fight against them with the sword of My mouth. He who has an ear, let him hear what the Spirit says to the churches. To him who overcomes I will give some of the hidden manna to eat. And I will give him a white stone, and on the stone a new name written which no one knows except him who receives it."

Pergamum was an ancient city in the region of Mysia in western Asia Minor. The modern day village of Bergama, Turkey now covers part of the ancient city. The site was occupied from the earliest recorded time, but became most famous in the third century B.C. At that time Pergamum became the center of an independent kingdom with impressive cultural achievements. King Eumenes II (197B.C. to 159B.C.) founded a library second only to that of Ptolemy Philadelphus in Alexandria. Pergamum also had a famous school of sculpture. Its wealth was based on agriculture surplus, silver mines, stock breeding, woolen textiles and the making of parchment.

Pergamum was one of the most beautiful Greek cities. Its public buildings were built on terraces on a steep mountain and culminated in the palace and fortifications at the Acropolis. In 133B.C. the last king to reign in Pergamum, Attalus III, bequeathed his kingdom to the Romans, which also included parts of Phrygia, Ionia, Caria, Lydia and Mysia. After his death it was made into the Roman province of Asia, with Pergamum as its capital. Under Augustus Caesar, Ephesus became the new capital. During the Roman period, a shrine to Asclepius, the Greek god of healing, was built in the lower city. It was a kind of spa at which both natural and supernatural modes of healing were used.

Verse 13 reveals that Pergamum is the place where Satan's throne was located and links Satan to Rome. Pergamum was one of the cities where the governor regularly held court and he alone held the right of capital punishment. Pergamum was called *Satan's throne* because it was one of the oldest and most prominent centers of imperial cult, i.e., the worship of the Roman emperor as a divine being.

In Revelation 1:16 John described the person who he saw speaking to him from the midst of the seven golden candlesticks. One of the features of this person was *"Out of his mouth went a sharp two-edged sword"*. In *Revelation 2:12* Jesus clearly defines Himself as the one with the two-edged sword.

In Greek the word sword used here is rhomphaia which means a saber or a long and broad cutlass. This two-edged sword which Christ is wielding is not a weapon formed by mortal man, but by our eternal, immortal Lord and savior Jesus Christ. Scripture tells us this two edged sword is the *word of God* and unless you have the Holy Spirit within you, you will not be able to wield this weapon properly against your adversary the devil. No evil, no enemy can stand against the word of God.

> *"Take the helmet of salvation, and the sword of the Spirit, which is the word of God."(Ephesians 6:17)*

> *"For the word of God is quick, and powerful, and sharper than any two-edged sword, piercing even to the dividing asunder of soul and spirit, and of the joints and marrow, and is a discerner of the thoughts and intents of the heart."(Hebrews 4:12)*

Christ says *"I know your works"*. It may be possible to hide things from your fellow man, but you cannot hide anything from God.

Christ continues *"And where you live, where Satan's throne is."* Christ is reassuring these people that He knows living in Pergamum was the worse place on earth at the time for a Christian.

[SEE ALSO: EPHESIANS 6:12]

Even though these people lived in the middle of evil, corruption and satanic influence, Christ reassures them that He knows they are holding on to His name and are refusing to give in to the wickedness and temptation which surrounds them. They have kept their faith and Christ says He is pleased with them for doing so. He says even though He is pleased with them for the above mentioned things, He still has: *"a few things against you, because you have there those who hold the doctrine of Balaam, who taught Balak to put a stumbling block before the children of Israel, to eat things sacrificed to idols, and to commit sexual immorality."*

The entire account of what took place between Balaam and Balac can be found in the Book of Numbers 22 - 25, & 31.

Balaam, a prophet, taught Israel's enemies, King Balac and the people of Moab that they could defeat Israel by introducing them to sexual immorality, eating meat sacrificed to false idols and by convincing them they could do God's work for a price.

[SEE ALSO: ACTS 15:29; II PETER 2:15-17; I CORINTHIANS 6:13-20; JUDE 11]

Nicolaitanes practiced and preached the eating of food sacrificed to idols and for promoting sexual freedom and adultery. They preached that since they were saved they were free to do whatever they wanted no matter how perverted.

Christ says he hates that doctrine, those who preach it and those who practice it. Christ gave the same warning to the church of Ephesus in Revelation 2:6.

Jesus urges us to repent or He will *"come quickly"* and *"fight against them with the sword of His mouth."* This is the weapon that we should wield against the enemy, *"the two-edged sword which is the word of God."*

The Lord closes the letter to the church of Pergamos with *"He that has an ear, let him hear what the Spirit says to the churches;"* (notice how the Lord's closing remark at the end of each letter is to all *churches* and not just to the individual church). The Lord warns us throughout scripture that there will be people who hearing God's word will still act deaf towards it, and seeing God's word in action, will still choose to not see it for what it really is.

[SEE ALSO: PSALMS 13:3; PSALMS 19:8; ISAIAH 6:9&10; EZEKIEL 12:1&2; MATTHEW 13:14&15; JOHN 8:43-47]

Christ reveals to us why He wants His children to keep their eyes and ears open.

> *"That the God of our Lord Jesus Christ, the Father of glory, may give to you the spirit of wisdom and revelation in the knowledge of Him the eyes of your understanding being enlightened; that you may know what is the hope of His calling, what are the riches of the glory of His inheritance in the saints, and what is the exceeding greatness of His power toward us who believe, according to the working of His mighty power which He worked in Christ when He raised Him from the dead and seated Him at His right hand in the heavenly places, far above all principality and power and might and dominion, and every name that is named, not only in this age but also in that which is to come. And He put all things under His feet, and gave Him to be head over all things to the church, which is His body, the fullness of Him who fills all in all." (Ephesians 1:17-23) (NKJV)*

God fed the Israelites manna in the dessert every day for 40 years. This is not a fairytale someone made up to amuse their child. God really did that. He wants us to eat also of the hidden manna, the Bread of Life, which is a relationship with Jesus Christ.

> "Jesus said to them, I tell you the truth it is not Moses who has given you the bread from heaven, but it is My Father who gives you the true bread from heaven. For the bread of God is He who comes down from heaven and gives life to the world." (John 6:32&33)(NIV)

> Jesus says: "I am the bread of life. He who comes to Me shall never hunger, and he who believes in Me shall never thirst." (John 6:35)

[SEE ALSO: JOHN 6:47-51]

Revelation 2:17c

> "And I will give him a white stone, and on the stone a new name written which no one knows except him who receives it."

Stones were used by the Pharisees and Sadducees for casting votes when someone was on trial. A black stone meant "guilty" and a white stone meant "not guilty". The accused person then carried the white stone with him to show his innocence to others.

When the Lord calls us home to be with Him, we will each get a white stone with our new name written on it to show that we are innocent from our sins through the shed blood of Christ Jesus. The only one who will know your new name is you and Christ who knew you before the foundations of the earth were formed.

[SEE ALSO: EPHESIANS 1:4]

Chapter 2

Church of Thyatira

Revelation 2:18-29

> "And to the angel of the church in Thyatira write, "These things say the Son of God, who has eyes like a flame of fire, and His feet like fine brass: I know your works, love, service, faith, and your patience; and as for your works, the last are more than the first. Nevertheless I have a few things against you, because you allow that woman Jezebel, who calls herself a prophetess, to teach and beguile My servants to commit sexual immorality and to eat things sacrificed to idols. And I gave her time to repent of her sexual immorality; and she did not repent. Indeed, I will cast her into a sickbed, and those who commit adultery with her into great tribulation, unless they repent of their deeds. And I will kill her children with death. And all the churches shall know that I am He who searches the minds and hearts. And I will give to each one of you according to your works. But to you I say, and to the rest in Thyatira, as many as do not have this doctrine, and who have not known the depths of Satan, as they call them, I will put on you no other burden. But hold fast what you have till I come. And he who overcomes, and keeps My works until the end, to him I will give power over the nations- 'He shall rule them with a rod of iron; as the potter's vessels shall be broken to pieces'- as I also have received from My Father; and I will give him the morning star. He who has an ear, let him hear what the Spirit says to the churches."

Thyatira is modern day Akhisar, located about 55 miles northeast of Izmir (Smyrna), Turkey. It lies on the road between Pergamum and

Sardis in Lydia (Mysia) on the Lycus River about 40 miles southeast of Pergamum. Founded as a Hellenistic city by Seleucus I Nicator in 300B.C. it developed many industrial and commercial guilds by the first century A.D. which required their members to participate in pagan celebration dedicated to pagan gods. By the late first century, a significant Christian community existed in Thyatira to merit the longest of the seven letters to the churches in Revelation. Christians in Thyatira were faced with the decision to either compromise their belief in the Lord and participate in some of the pagan festivities, or suffer economic hardship.

Christ commended the church at Thyatira for its good works charity and strong faith but they were still missing the main point. The emphasis is on their works, it is the first commendation and the last commendation mentioned.

[SEE ALSO: ROMANS 4:2-5; 6:23; GALATIANS 2:16; EPHESIANS 2: 8&9]

Christ also had a horrible complaint against them because of their complacency allowing Jezebel a teacher to teach false doctrine in the church. Jezebel typified the system of the "papal church". When the Roman Catholic Church introduced images, statues and pictures for the people to bow down to, light candles to and pray to, it began the practice of idolatry. When it claimed that the teachings and doctrines of the church are superior to the Word of God, it assumed the role of a prophetess.

A study of the Papal System from 606A.D. to the reformation in 1520A.D. (also known as the Dark Ages), with its institution of the "sacrifice of the mass" and other pagan rights, reveals the sway of Jezebel. It was also a period of persecution as seen in the wars of the Crusades and the rise of the inquisition. The medieval papal church headed by Rome, "in the name of Jesus", conquered lands, plundered villages and converted many to their idolatrous system. Jezebel falsely taught the church they could live pagan, sexually immoral lifestyles and still be Christians.

Christ in His loving mercy, patience and long suffering, gave this woman Jezebel and her corrupt system a chance to repent and receive forgiveness. Today in the 21st century He is leaving the door open for the Papal system to repent, return to Jesus Christ and acknowledge Him as the one and only true God, and the Scriptures as the only true word of God.

Christ is patient and long suffering with us as well. He is giving us a chance to repent and receive forgiveness.

The Scriptures say *"WOE to those who refuse to believe the truth. They will have to pass through the Great Tribulation"* (Revelation 6-19), or the *"White Throne Judgment"* (Revelation 20:11-15) or both. Christ tells us that in the end He will destroy all those who have refused to acknowledge Him as Lord and Savior. He knows our hearts. He knows who truly believes and who doesn't. Do you believe? Those who believe in Him receive everlasting life. That's a promise from Him. Those who don't believe will be cast into the Lake of Fire with the devil and his angels, for all eternity. That's also a promise from the Lord.

[SEE ALSO: MATTHEW 25:41; REVELATION 12:9; 20:11-15]

God is merciful. He gives these people a stern warning but shows His grace and mercy at the same time. If they refuse to follow this doctrine of Jezebel and keep from doing Satan's bidding (idol worship, fornication, sexual immorality) He will put no other burden on them.

Revelation 2:25

"But hold fast what you have till I come."

Jesus is coming back.

Revelation 2:26

> "And he who overcomes, and keeps My works until the end, to him I will give power over the nations."

Doing good works for Christ does not get you to heaven, but it does earn you crowns. Overcoming means to abide in Christ.

[SEE ALSO: EPHESIANS 2:10; II TIMOTHY 3:16&17; TITUS 2:13&14]

We will rule with Christ when He comes back to the earth, and there will be no nonsense, no deceit, no taking bribes or doing special favors for only certain people. We will rule and reign with Christ in total 100% truth and honesty. The liars, cheaters etc. will be destroyed.

[SEE ALSO: ISAIAH 29:15&16; 41:25; 45:9; 64:8]

Christ's desire is that no one be lost.

> "For God so loved the world that He gave His only begotten Son, that whosoever believeth in Him should not perish, but have everlasting life. For God sent not His Son into the world to condemn the world; but that the world through Him might be saved."(John 3:16&17)

God wants churches in this 21st century to wake up and listen to what He has to say before it's too late.

CHAPTER 3

CHURCH OF SARDIS

Revelation 3:1-6

> *"And to the angel of the church in Sardis write, 'These things says He who has the seven Spirits of God and the seven stars: I know your works, that you have a name that you are alive, but you are dead. Be watchful, and strengthen the things which remain, that are ready to die, for I have not found your works perfect before God. Remember therefore how you have received and heard; hold fast and repent. Therefore if you will not watch, I will come upon you as a thief, and you will not know what hour I will come upon you. You have a few names even in Sardis who have not defiled their garments; and they shall walk with Me in white, for they are worthy. He who overcomes shall be clothed in white garments, and I will not blot out his name from the Book of Life; but I will confess his name before My Father and before His angels. He who has an ear, let him hear what the Spirit says to the churches."*

Sardis, located on the slope of Mount Tumulus, the capital city of Lydia in the province of Asia Minor was almost impregnable. The city was founded in the third century B.C. and Greek was the native dialect. The Lydian kings revered the Greek gods, were benefactors of Hellanic sanctuaries and consulted the oracle at Delphi. In Roman times, Sardis was the center of the imperial cult. When John was writing this book, Sardis was ruled by the monarch Croesus and was home to the Greek philosopher, Thales. This easily defended city fell to invading armies twice because the defenders left the walls unguarded.

Sardis, noted for its carpet industry, was a wealthy city that was destroyed by an earthquake.

The church at Sardis was well known and well attended because of its good works, but it was dead because it did not know Christ spiritually. It was given over to ritualistic worship. It appeared godly but without the power because of the lack of deep hearted devotion to the Lord.
[see also: Colossians 2:13]

The word Sardis means "escaping one" or those who "come out". This is an excellent example of the church in the "reformation period" which officially started October 31, 1517 A.D. when Martin Luther nailed his 95 theses on the church door at Wittenberg, Germany and a number of other reformers also protested against the tyranny and false teachings of the papal church. Unfortunately it became more a struggle for political liberty rather than a purely Christian movement. It caused such a multiplication of sects that it brought about bitter controversy to the point that it could be truly said: *"You have a reputation of being alive, but you are dead" (Revelation 3:1 NIV).* To this day churches of different denominations are doing *good works* but argue over doctrine. Many are dead, even though they may be well known and popular.

The church at Sardis received the shortest commendation from our Lord of any of the seven churches. He starts verse two by telling

them to be *"watchful"*. The Lord uses the word "watch" and "be watchful" to tell us that as Christians we should always be watching for His return. We should always act in a manner that if He came back for us today we would not be ashamed or embarrassed.
[SEE ALSO: MATTHEW 24:36&42; 25:13; LUKE 12:39; ACTS 1:7; I THESSALONIANS 5:1&2; II PETER 3:10]

The Lord says to the church of Sardis: *"strengthen the things which remain, that are ready to die."* Christ is telling them whatever teachings, scripture and spiritual truths they have, they need to hold unto them, strengthen their faith and belief in them and not allow false doctrine and rituals to spiritually kill them. Christ continues with *"For I have not found your works perfect before God"*. In the Greek language the word *perfect* means "complete". The Lord is admonishing them because even though they are doing good works, they are lacking in the faith that is necessary to support the works.

> *"This also faith by itself, if it does not have works, is dead. But someone will say, "You have faith, and I have works." Show me your faith without your works, and I will show you my faith by my works. You believe there is one God. You do well. Even the demons believe - and tremble! But do you want to know, O foolish man, that faith without works is dead?"(James 2:17-20)*

The people of this church were doing good works for others but expecting something back in return. Obviously their motives were impure and their actions were not done in love. Unfortunately many people and churches today are similar.
[SEE ALSO: COLOSSIANS 3:23-25]

Jesus reminds the people of the church of Sardis that they received His word from those who were eye witnesses to His activities on this earth and from the apostle Paul with whom God divinely intervened. He told them to hold fast to those teachings and spiritual truths that were taught them and repent.

Repent means to "turn away from". Jesus is telling the church and us to turn away from idol and ritualistic worship and to come back to Him and to His word which is truth. An idol is anything in your life that you put ahead of God. God has to be first in everything you say, do and think.

[SEE ALSO: MATTHEW 3:1&2; 4:17; MARK 1:15; 6:12; LUKE 13:2-5; ACTS 2:38]

Jesus warns us not to be caught unaware. We should be watching for His coming, because when He comes it will be quick *(Matthew 24:36)*. Only His Father knew the time because Jesus had put aside His deity when He became man. After Christ was crucified and rose from the dead, Jesus tells us that: *"All power is given to Me in heaven and on earth"* (Matthew 28:18). Once Christ completed everything the Father sent Him to do He turned over all things to His Son Jesus, including the "hour and the day."

Revelation 3:3 reveals that Christ's message to the churches about His coming back gets more urgent as He moves from church to church.

> Revelation2:5 To Ephesus: *"I will come to you quickly"*
>
> Revelation 2:16 To Pergamum: *"Repent, or else I will come to you quickly"*
>
> Revelation 3:3 To Sardis: *"I will come upon you as a thief"*
>
> Revelation 3:11 To Philadelphia: *"Behold, I come quickly"*
>
> Revelation 3:20 To Laodicea: *"I stand at the door and knock"* (21st century church)

As in all the churches and church ages throughout history, there always exists a remnant who will be faithful to the Lord. They believe the scriptures are truth.

REVELATION 3:5

> *"He who overcomes shall be clothed in white garments, and I will not blot out his name from the Book of Life; but I will confess his name before My Father and before His angels."*

To get "blotted out" of the Book of Life, means you must have "been in it". At birth your name is written in the "Book of Life" but when you commit your first willful sin, you cut yourself off from God and your name gets blotted out. To get your name back into the Book of Life you must accept Jesus Christ as your Lord and Savior. This means admitting you are a sinner. Sin cuts you off from God. Jesus sacrificed his life on the cross as atonement for our sins. You must repent of your sins. Commit to turn away from the behaviors that are sinful and turn to Jesus as the leader of your life. Being good and kind and generous is not enough. You must acknowledge that only through the sacrifice of Jesus shed blood on the cross you can have eternal life.

[SEE ALSO: ROMANS 8:38&39]

You cannot lose your salvation and no one can take it from you, not even Satan.

This does not mean however you cannot use your own free will to give your salvation up freely. Just as God will not force anyone to accept Jesus Christ, He will not force anybody to reject Him. We have free will and the right to choose life or death. Scripture shows us a Christian can be blotted out from the Book of Life if that's what he/she so chooses. This happens by committing the *unpardonable sin* which scripture says is "Blasphemy of the Holy Spirit" this is to completely turn your back on God, denounce Him and His existence and reject His Son Jesus Christ. Doing so is not only sinning in the flesh, but sinning in the spirit. It is taking the Holy Spirit dwelling in you and kicking Him out. That is the *sin unto death*.

"I tell you the truth, all the sins and blasphemes of men will be forgiven them. But whoever blasphemes against the Holy Spirit will never be forgiven: he is guilty of an eternal sin." (Mark 3:28&29)(NIV)

[SEE ALSO: I JOHN 5:16; HEBREWS 6:4-6; 10:26]

Revelation 3:5c

"I will confess his name before My Father and before His angels."

This scripture is very clear and easy to understand. "Whosoever therefore shall confess Me before men, him will I confess also before My Father which is in heaven. But whosoever shall deny Me before men, him will I also deny before My Father which is in heaven." (Matthew 10:32&33)

[SEE ALSO: LUKE 9:26]

Revelation 3:6

"He who has an ear, let him hear what the Spirit says to the churches."

We must keep our spiritual ears open so when the Holy Spirit speaks to us we can listen and understand what he is trying to tell us. This does not necessarily mean you will hear an audible voice but if you open your heart and mind to the Holy Spirit's leading, you will know when he is directing you.

[SEE ALSO: MARK 8:38; LUKE 12:8&9; II TIMOTHY 2:11&12; I JOHN 2:22&23;]

CHURCH OF PHILADELPHIA

Revelation 3:7-13

"And to the angel of the church in Philadelphia write, 'These things says He who is holy, He who is true, "He who has the key of David, He who opens and no one shuts, and shuts and *no one opens": I know your works. See, I have set before you an open door, and no one can shut it; for you have a little strength, have kept My word, and have not denied My name. Indeed I will make those of the synagogue of Satan, who say they are Jews and are not, but lie-indeed I will make them come and worship before your feet, and to know that I have loved you. Because you have kept My command to persevere, I also will keep you from the hour of trial which shall come upon the whole world, to test those who dwell on the earth. Behold, I come quickly! Hold fast what you have, that no one may take your crown. He who overcomes, I will make him a pillar in the temple of My God, and he shall go out no more. And I will write on him the name of My God and the name of the city of My God, the New Jerusalem, which comes down out of heaven from My God. And I will write on him My new name. He who has an ear, let him hear what the Spirit says to the churches.'"*

Philadelphia is the modern day city of Alashehir (The City of God), Turkey, in the region of Lydia in western Asia Minor. It is twenty five miles south east of the city of Sardis on an eight-hundred foot rise. Philadelphia founded by Attalus II, King of Pergamum (159B.C.-138B.C.) is also known as "Little Athens" because of the pagan temples and festivals held there. As the center for the textile industry, agriculture and leather production, its strategic location made it a critical link in trade and communication between Laodicea and Hierapolis to the east of it and Sardis and Pergamum to the west.

Of the seven churches mentioned in Revelation, only the church of Philadelphia (brotherly love) has the right to free Christian worship, a privilege which is not allowed in any other inland city of Asia Minor today. Their spiritual faithfulness down through the centuries has blessed them.

Revelation 3:7b

"He that is Holy"

It is one of Christ's many divine titles. He is the Holy of holies.

[SEE ALSO: PSALMS 30:4; 89:18; ISAIAH 6:3; ACTS 3:14&15]

Revelation 3:7b

"He that is true"

Another divine title, He is truth and cannot lie.

[SEE ALSO: JOHN 14:6; I JOHN 5:20]

Revelation 3:7c&8

"He that has the key of David, He that opens and no man shuts, and shuts and no one opens. I know your works. See, I have set before you an open door, and no one can shut it; for you have a little strength, have kept my word, and have not denied my name."

"And the key of the house of David will I lay upon His shoulder, so He shall open, and none shall shut, and He shall shut, and none shall open."(Isaiah 22:22)

[SEE ALSO: LUKE 1:31-33; REVELATION 3:20]

Unlike the previous churches, the works the church of Philadelphia was doing were righteous. They kept Jesus first in their lives and all their works edified Him, not themselves. Because of the great works of the Philadelphia church, Christ opened the door for them. This church was like a person regaining full strength when on the verge of death. It was a dead church being revived, and revivals were characteristic of the Philadelphia period. Revivals began in 1739A.D. with men such as George Whitefield and followed by John Wesley, Charles G. Finney and D.L. Moody.

The people of the church of Philadelphia did not deny Christ despite torture and martyrdom.

[SEE ALSO: ROMANS 10:9-11]

REVELATION 3:9

> "Indeed I will make those of the synagogue of Satan, who say they are Jews and are not, but lie – indeed I will make them come and worship before your feet, and to know that I have loved you."

The Jews who were persecuting the Christians aren't real Jews (in their heart and spirit) but of Satan's synagogue. These Jews questioned the authority of the gospels. They felt they alone were God's chosen people. They only accepted the Old Testament as the inspired word of God.

One who God considers a true Jew today, is not one who is a Jew outwardly (circumcised), but one who is internally circumcised (in the heart) and believes Jesus is who he proclaimed to be.

> "For he is not a Jew who is one outwardly, nor is that circumcision which is outward in the flesh; but he is a Jew who is one inwardly, and circumcision is that of the heart, in the Spirit, and not in the letter; whose praise is not from men but from God." (Romans 2:28&29)

Jesus says that He will make these lying Jews of Satan's synagogue come and worship at the feet of the true believers.

> "Thus says the Lord God: "Behold, I will lift My hand in an oath to the nations, and set up My standard for the peoples; they shall bring your sons in their arms, and your daughters shall be carried on their shoulders; kings shall be your foster fathers, and their queens your nursing mothers; they shall bow down to you with their faces to the earth, and

> lick up the dust of your feet. Then you will know that I am the LORD, for they shall not be ashamed who wait for Me." (Isaiah 49:22&23)

[SEE ALSO: ISAIAH 60:14]

REVELATION 3:10

> "Because you have kept my command to persevere, I also will keep you from the hour of trial which shall come upon the whole world, to test those who dwell on the Earth."

What kind of a just God would He be, if believers would have to go through the "wrath of God" the same as unbelievers?

> "But God demonstrates His own love toward us, in that while we were still sinners, Christ died for us. Much more then, having now been justified by His blood, we shall be saved from wrath through Him." (Romans 5:8&9)

> "For God did not appoint us to wrath, but to obtain salvation through our Lord Jesus Christ, who died for us, that whether we wake or sleep, we should live together with Him." (I Thessalonians 5:9&10)

[SEE ALSO: EZRA 8:22B; ISAIAH 13:9&13; NAHUM 1:2; ZEPHANIAH 1:14-18; MALACHI 4:1; ROMANS 2:5; I THESSALONIANS 1:10; II PETER 2:9]

The above scriptures are clear that believers of Jesus Christ will not go through the *great tribulation* which is the wrath of God.

REVELATION 3:11

> "Behold, I come quickly! Hold fast what you have, that no one may take your crown."

"I will come quickly" the Greek word "Tachu", means "without delay, by surprise, suddenly". Nothing further needs to happen in scripture before Jesus calls for His church to meet Him in the air.

> "But I do not want you to be ignorant, brethren, concerning those who have fallen asleep, lest you sorrow as others who have no hope. For if we believe that Jesus died and rose again, even so God will bring with Him those who sleep in Jesus. For this we say to you by the word of the Lord, that we who are alive and remain until the coming of the Lord will by no means precede those who are asleep. For the Lord himself will descend from heaven with a shout, with the voice of an archangel, and with the trumpet of God. And the dead in Christ will rise first. Then we who are alive and remain shall be caught up together with them in the clouds to meet the Lord in the air. And thus we shall always be with the Lord. Therefore comfort one another with these words."
> (I Thessalonians 4:13-18)

[SEE ALSO: I CORINTHIANS 15:51-58; I THESSALONIANS 5:2]

There are five types of crowns spoken of in Scripture which believers can earn:

1. Crown of Glory (I Peter 5:4)
2. Crown of Rejoicing (I Thessalonians 2:19)
3. Crown of Righteousness (II Timothy 4:8)
4. Crown of Life (James 1:12)
5. Crown of Gold (Revelation 4:4)

Revelation 3:12

> "He who overcomes, I will make him a pillar in the Temple of my God, and he shall go out no more. And I will write on him the name of my God and the name of the city of my God, and the new Jerusalem, which comes down out of heaven from my God. And I will write on him my new name."

Jesus says those *"that overcome"* He will make them *"pillars"* in God's temple. In Greek the word *pillar* is "stulos" which means "a type of support" (figuratively). Because these believers stand firm in the word of God and never deny Jesus, He will use them in His temple.

> Paul wrote to Timothy: *"But if I am delayed I write so that you may know how you ought to conduct yourself in the house of God, which is the church of the living God, the pillar and ground of the truth."* (I Timothy 3:15)

> *"James, Peter, and John, those reputed to be pillars, gave me and Barnabas the right hand of fellowship when they recognized the grace given to me. They agreed that we should go to the Gentiles, and they to the Jews."* (Galatians 2:9) (NIV)

The over comers will be given three new names:

1. The name of God
2. The name of the city of God which is New Jerusalem
3. Jesus new name

REVELATION 3:13

> *"He who has an ear, let him hear what the Spirit says to the churches."*

Listen to the Lord, keep His word, profess His name and avoid the wrath to come.

CHURCH OF LAODICEA

Revelation 3:14-22

> *"And to the angel of the church of the Laodiceans write, 'These things say the Amen, the Faithful and True Witness,*

the Beginning of the creation of God: I know your works, that you are neither cold nor hot. I could wish you were cold or hot. So then, because you are lukewarm, and neither cold nor hot, I will spew you out of My mouth. Because you say, I am rich, have become wealthy, and have need of nothing'- and do not know that you art wretched, miserable, poor, blind, and naked- I counsel you to buy from Me gold refined in the fire, that you may be rich; and white garments, that you may be clothed, that the shame of your nakedness may not be revealed; and anoint your eyes with eye salve, that you may see. As many as I love, I rebuke and chasten. Therefore be zealous and repent. Behold, I stand at the door and knock. If anyone hears My voice and opens the door, I will come in to him and dine with him, and he with Me. To him who overcomes I will grant to sit with Me on My throne, as I also overcame and sat down with My Father on His throne. He who has an ear, let him hear what the Spirit says to the churches.'"

Laodicea was a prosperous, commercial city in the region of Phrygia in northwest Asia Minor located forty five miles southeast of Philadelphia. It was famous for its wool distribution, production of eye ointment, medicine, banking and manufacturing. Situated on a plateau in the South of the Lycus River Valley, Antiochus II of the Seleucid dynasty named the city after his wife, Laodice.

The church of Laodicea was very rich materially, but very poor spiritually.

Revelation 3:14b

"These things say the Amen, the Faithful and True witness."

Jesus is the finality of God's word. He is the seal, the *Amen* to all that is written which can not be changed.

> "For assuredly, I say to you, Till heaven and earth pass away, one jot or one tittle will by no means pass from the law till all is fulfilled." (Matthew 5:18)

In Hebrew, Amen (aw-mane) means; sure, truly, truth, so be it. In Greek, Amen (am-ane) means; firm, trustworthy, surely as in "so be it", verily (truly).

[SEE ALSO: JOHN 8:14; REVELATION 1:5A]

Revelation 3:14c

> "The Beginning of the creation of God"

The Greek word for beginning used here is "arche" (ar-khay) and means chief, magistrate, power, rule, source, or origin. Jesus is the "Alpha"-the creator of the very first thing that was ever created. Jesus is the "Omega"- the creator of the very last thing that was or ever will be created. Jesus created and spoke everything into existence so He Himself already had to be in existence. Jesus created the beginning and the end of everything, but He, Himself, always was, is and will be.

> "In the beginning, was the Word (Jesus), and the Word (Jesus) was with God, and the Word (Jesus) was (is) God. The same was in the beginning with God." (John 1:1&2)

[SEE ALSO: PROVERBS 8:22&23; COLOSSIANS 1:15-18]

REVELATION 3:15&16

> "I know your works, that you are neither cold nor hot. I could wish you were cold or hot. So then, because you are lukewarm, and neither cold nor hot, I will spew you out of my mouth."

It is interesting to see how God reprimanded the Laodicean church using the example of "lukewarm". The city of Laodicea received its water through an aqueduct four miles away. The waters from the city of Hierapolis were famous for their hot springs but by the time the water reached Laodicea, the water was "lukewarm" neither cold enough to be a refreshing drink nor hot enough to be a restorative bath.

> Jesus will not tolerate a lukewarm church. "And Elijah came to all the people, and said, "How long will you falter between two opinions? If the LORD is God, follow Him; but if Baal, then follow him." But the people answered him not a word." (I Kings 18:21)

[SEE ALSO: MATTHEW 6:24; LUKE 16:13]

The Lord says He will "spew" (spit) out of His mouth those who are lukewarm. "Spew" in the Greek language is *emeo* (em-eh-o) and means to "vomit". The Lord is so disgusted with lukewarm people who say they are believers but do not follow His word. They are considered to be "vomit" and He will treat them as such. God's judgment will be certain. There will be no middle ground when He judges. It will be either heaven or hell. Unfortunately today many of our churches are in this "lukewarm" condition. There is much going on in them, but more is of a social nature rather than a spiritual nature. The cause of this lukewarm condition is self-deception.

In Revelation 3:17 Jesus related the condition of the church to the quality of the city. The people of Laodicea felt they were in need of nothing. They bragged about their material riches, but were spiritually poor. They were famous for their eye salve, yet Christ said they were spiritually blind. They were known for their superb wool, but were spiritually naked.

Many churches today think they can do nothing without money. The truth is that we can do nothing without Christ. The world cannot be converted by money, but only by the Spirit of God.

Revelation 3:18a

> "I counsel you to buy from Me gold refined in the fire."

God indicates faithfulness to him is worth more than gold and cannot be bought. The Laodiceans needed righteousness.

[SEE ALSO: PSALMS 12:6; 19:9&10; ZECHARIAH 13:9; I PETER 1:7]

Revelation 3:18b

> "And white garments, that you may be clothed, that the shame of your nakedness may not be revealed."

White garments are a sign of true and pure righteousness; righteous living, something that was lacking in Laodicea.

The church of Laodicea was "naked". Their outward garments were made of the finest material and fashion for the time because they were noted for their wool industry. But Christ counseled them to purchase His "white raiment", instead of the "raven black" wool that the Laodicean garment makers were famous for.

REVELATION 3:18c

> "And anoint your eyes with eye salve that you may see."

The church of Laodicea was spiritually blind. They could see their worldly prosperity, but were blind to the heavenly prosperity. The Lord counseled them to cleanse their eyes spiritually so they could clearly differentiate between what is of man and what is of God. The merchants of Laodicea dealt in eye ointments that had a high degree of healing power, but had no salve that could restore impaired spiritual vision. Only the healing power of Jesus Christ through their repentance could give this church the sight they lacked.

REVELATION 3:19&20

> *"As many as I love, I rebuke and chasten. Therefore be zealous and repent. Behold, I stand at the door and knock. If anyone hears My voice and opens the door, I will come in to him and dine with him and he with Me."*

The words: *"Behold, I stand at the door, and knock: if any man hears My voice, and opens the door, I will come in to him, and will sup with him, and he with Me"* are usually quoted as an appeal to an individual sinner. But here, Christ addresses it to an entire church, a church in which Christ once stood in the midst of *(Revelation 1:12&13)*, and now finds Himself standing outside looking in. Christ is appealing to one lukewarm member at a time to open up the door to their heart and reignite their fire for the Lord.

REVELATION 3:21&22

> *"To him who overcomes I will grant to sit with Me on My throne, as I also overcame and sat down with My Father on His throne. He who has an ear, let him hear what the Spirit says to the churches."*

The Laodicea overcomers are promised to reign with Christ as part of His body. Jesus pleads with these people to open the spiritual ears of their hearts so they might be saved.

CHAPTER 4

Revelation 4:1

> *"After these things I looked, and behold, a door standing open in heaven. And the first voice which I heard was like a trumpet speaking with me, saying, "Come up here, and I will show you things which must take place after this."*

After John received the messages to the churches, he looked and saw the door to heaven open and God calling him up to heaven. John's spirit ascended to the throne of God. The voice tells John to *"Come up here"*. John being called up to heaven is symbolic of Christ's church (His bride) being called up to heaven which is known as the *rapture*. From this point on when the church is talked about in Revelation, it is in heaven, not on the earth.

The Lord is about to reveal to John the future of mankind.

Revelation 4:2&3

> *"Immediately I was in the Spirit: and behold, a throne set in heaven, and One sat on the throne. And He who sat there was like a jasper and a sardius stone in appearance; and there was a rainbow around the throne, in appearance like an emerald."*

The first thing John sees is the throne of God, and God Himself in all His glory sitting on it. The throne is the key to this fourth chapter. Everything is centered on the throne which is mentioned 46 times in the Book of Revelation.

John describes the Glory of God looking like a jasper stone (a clear polished gem like a diamond). John saw what looked like a gigantic diamond sparkling in brilliance, representing the *glory of God*, and a blood red sardine stone like a ruby which symbolizes the *blood of Christ* and reminds us of the sacrifice Christ made for us at the cross. There was an emerald rainbow around the throne. Emerald is the stone of the tribe of Judah from which Jesus is a descendent. This is not the type of rainbow that we see after a rain storm, but a completely circular rainbow representing the eternal nature of God, much like a wedding band having no beginning or end and symbolizing never ending love in a marriage. The circular rainbow symbolizes life and eternity.

Revelation 4:4

> "And round about the throne were four and twenty seats: and upon the seats I saw four and twenty elders sitting, clothed in white raiment; and they had on their heads crowns of gold."

The twenty four elders represent redeemed mankind. The term "elder" is never applied to angels. Angels do not have crowns or sit on thrones. Only redeemed people are promised thrones and crowns.

[SEE ALSO: MATTHEW 19:28; LUKE 22:28-30]

These elders are representatives of the Old and New Testament saints which have been redeemed by the blood of Christ. In the Book of Daniel, the seats were not yet occupied.

Twenty four is the number of priestly portions as shown in the Old Testament. In I Chronicles 24:1-19 King David divided the priests into divisions. He found there were 24 leaders of the priestly families (Levites). He made these 24 leaders representatives of the entire priesthood which consisted of thousands of priests.

The Old Testament saints are represented by the twelve tribes of Israel, and the New Testament saints by the twelve apostles. Together these make up 24 representative characters. This is clearly illustrated in the description of the New Jerusalem, where the twelve foundation stones are named after the twelve apostles and the twelve gates after the twelve tribes of Israel in Revelation 21:10-14.

The Old Testament saints are the *friends* of the bridegroom (Jesus); they are the *appointed guests* at the marriage feast of the Lamb.

> John 3:29 John the Baptist said: *"He who has the bride is the bridegroom: but the friend of the bridegroom, who stands and hears Him, rejoices greatly because of the bridegroom's voice. Therefore this joy of mine is fulfilled."*

Revelation 4:5a

> *"And from the throne proceeded lightnings, thunderings, and voices."*

The voices are coming directly from the throne. It could be the Godhead speaking or the Seraphim, guardians of the throne, which are a separate class of angels and considered to be "living creatures" in Scripture.

Revelation 4:5b

> *"And there were seven lamps of fire burning before the throne, which are the seven Spirits of God."*

The number seven is alluded to as God's sacred number in the Scriptures. It symbolizes "perfection" or "completeness". The Greek word for *spirit* is pneuma (pnyoo-mah) and in this verse means "Divine God, Christ's Spirit and Holy Spirit". What John is revealing to us is God complete. The Seven Spirits represent God's character and personality, the Holy Spirit. John sees the Father, the Lamb (Jesus) and the Holy Spirit together at the throne which is commonly known as the *Trinity* although the term is not found in scripture.

The seven lamp stands of fire burning represent the Seven Spirits of God: *"And I looked, and behold, in the midst of the throne and of the four living creatures, and in the midst of the elders, stood a Lamb (Jesus) as though it had been slain, having seven horns (the all wise, all knowing, King of kings) and seven eyes (all seeing), which are the Seven Spirits of God sent out into all the earth."*

Isaiah 11:2 says the seven Spirits are:

1. Spirit of the LORD
2. Spirit of Wisdom
3. Spirit of Understanding
4. Spirit of Counsel
5. Spirit of Might
6. Spirit of Knowledge
7. Spirit of fear (respect) of the LORD

Revelation 4:6a

"Before the throne there was a sea of glass, like crystal."

There is no one on the sea of glass at this time. It is smooth and reflective as a mirror. The sea of glass is located in the outer court of the temple. The souls of the martyrs of the tribulation period are under the sea of glass at this time awaiting the end of the great tribulation. The tribulation saints and martyrs were not cleansed by fire baptism, so they will have to be purified by the Holy Spirit (fire baptism) in the outer court before they can enter the *holy place*. The high priest in Old Testament times had to purify himself before the brazen altar before he could enter the holy place to talk with God.

Revelation 4:6b-8

> "And in the midst of the throne, and around the throne, were four living creatures full of eyes in front and in back. The first living creature was like a lion, the second living creature like a calf, the third living creature had a face like a man, and the fourth living creature was like a flying eagle. And the four living creatures, each having six wings, were full of eyes around and within. And they do not rest day or night, saying: Holy, holy, holy, Lord God Almighty, who was and is and is to come!"

These are a distinguished class of angels called Seraphim. They are guardians of the throne of God and they go wherever the throne goes.

In *Numbers 2:1-34* the LORD gave Moses specific instructions how the camp of Israel should be set up with the twelve tribes. The camp of *Judah* on the east side was composed of three tribes (Judah, Zebulon, and Issachar) with its flag bearing the figure of a Lion (King of the Jews, Messiah). The camp of *Reuben* on the south side was composed of the three tribes (Reuben, Gad, and Simeon) with its flag bearing the figure of a Man (son of Adam). The camp of *Ephraim* on the west side was composed of the three tribes (Ephraim, Benjamin, and Manasseh) with its flag bearing the figure of an Ox (the servant). The camp of *Dan* on the north side was composed of the three tribes (Dan, Asher, and Naphtali) with its flag bearing the figure of an Eagle (heavenly origin). In the center of the camp was the tabernacle, the place of God's presence.

The four living creatures seem to also be attendants to the throne of God. They are the ones who summon the four horsemen in *Revelation 6:1-8*. One of them also hands the golden bowls filled with the wrath of God to the seven angels that pour out the bowls upon the Earth.

> *"Then one of the four living creatures gave to the seven angels seven golden bowls full of the wrath of God who lives forever and ever." (Revelation 15:7)*

The Seraphim never cease to praise God's holiness.

Revelation 4:9-11

> *"Whenever the living creatures give glory and honor and thanks to Him who sits on the throne, who lives forever and ever, the twenty-four elders fall down before Him who sits on the throne and worship Him who lives forever and ever, and cast their crowns before the throne, saying: 'You are worthy, O Lord, To receive glory and honor and power; for You created all things, And by Your will they exist and were created.'"*

When the living creatures give the glory, honor and thanks to God, it is a signal to the twenty four elders to fall down before the throne and give God worship. Through this they acknowledge that God is the only one worthy to receive glory, honor and power as creator of all things.

CHAPTER 5

Revelation 5:1

> *"And I saw in the right hand of Him who sat on the throne a scroll written inside and on the back, sealed with seven seals."*

The scroll was written on both the front and back sides then rolled up and sealed with a wax seal. This was done so that the person to whom the scroll was sent would know if it was tampered with before they received it. Roman law required wills to be validated by the seals of five or seven witnesses. Remember that seven is God's number of completeness. This scroll contains the total or complete judgment of the wrath of God to be poured out onto all the earth for their sin and disobedience which was the rejection of Jesus Christ as Lord and Savior.

Revelation 5:2&3

> *"Then I saw a strong angel proclaiming with a loud voice, "Who is worthy to open the scroll and to loose its seals?" And no one in heaven or on the earth or under the earth was able to open the scroll, or to look at it."*

John makes it a point of specifying that this was a strong angel and was the first of three strong angels which appear in Revelation

(Revelation 10:1 & 18:21). The call went out throughout the universe yet no one was worthy to open the scroll or even to look upon it. This book was held in the right hand of Almighty God. No one could look upon the book because the book with its seven seals is perfect judgment from a perfect God. There is no error in His judgment and therefore no room for dispute. Yet Jesus who is worthy and able to open the book did not answer the angel's question.

Revelation 5:4

> *"So I wept much, because no one was found worthy to open and read the scroll, or to look at it."*

John was in agony. No one, not one being in the entire universe could open the scroll.

Revelation 5:5

> *"But one of the elders said to me, "Do not weep. Behold, the Lion of the tribe of Judah, the Root of David, has prevailed to open the scroll and to loose its seven seals."*

The elder says to John *"behold the Lion"*, but to John's surprise when he looks he sees *"the Lamb"*. This shows Christ as both the humble servant (Lamb) and the King of kings (Lion). Scripture says Jesus is the *"Root of David"*:

> *"The days are coming," declares the LORD, when I will raise up to David a righteous Branch, a King who will reign wisely and do what is just and right in the land. In His days Judah will be saved and Israel will live in safety. This is the name by which He will be called; THE LORD OUR RIGHTEOUSNESS."* (Jeremiah 23:5&6)(NIV)

REVELATION 5:6

> *"and I looked, and behold, in the midst of the throne and of the four living creatures, and in the midst of the elders, stood a lamb as though it had been slain, having seven horns and seven eyes, which are the seven Spirits of God sent out into all the Earth."*

The seven Spirits of God reveals God's perfect character and perfect personality through Jesus Christ.

Jesus *prevailed* to open the book. "Prevailed" is from the same Greek word translated "overcome" in Revelation 2&3, *"nikao" (nik-ah-o)*.

Jesus the *Lamb*, in Greek is: *"arnion" (ar-nee-on)* and means a male lamb. It is used 29 times in Revelation to refer to Jesus. He is standing in this passage because he is about to take the scroll from the hand of God.

The horns are symbols of power and authority. In Hebrew the word is *"Qeren" (keh-ren)*. Jesus has absolute power and authority over everything and everybody.

The eyes signify insight, comprehension and watchfulness. The Greek word is *"opthalmos" (op-thal-mos)* which means vision. Jesus sees everything at all times, past, present and future. There is nothing we do that is secret from God.

The Seven Spirits of God symbolize God complete (Father, Son, Holy Spirit).

John 4:24 *"God is a Spirit and we worship Him in spirit and in truth."* The Greek word is *"pneuma" (pnyoo-mah)* and means "Divine God".

Revelation 5:7&8

> "Then He came and took the scroll out of the right hand of Him who sat on the throne. Now when He had taken the scroll, the four living creatures and the twenty-four elders fell down before the Lamb, each having a harp, and golden bowls full of incense, which are the prayers of the saints."

Jesus, the only one who is worthy, takes the scroll from His Father. Jesus created us, Jesus is the only one who died for us and therefore Jesus is the only one worthy to judge the earth that rejected Him.

As soon as Jesus takes the scroll out of His Father's hand the four beasts in the midst of the throne and the entire redeemed church (Christ's bride), symbolized by the twenty four elders, bow before the Lamb to worship Him. Each one has a harp. The prayers of the saints are so precious to God that they are put into golden bowls accompanied with the smell of beautiful sweet incense to be presented to our Lord.

Revelation 5:9

> "And they sang a new song, saying: "You are worthy to take the scroll, and to open its seals; for You were slain, and have redeemed us to God by Your blood out of every tribe and tongue and people and nation,"

The Lamb is worthy because He was slaughtered and paid the price for sinners.

"Tribe, tongue, people and nation" emphasize the diversity of the group purchased by the Lords death. No one particular nation, color, race, language or religion has an exclusive hold or ownership of Jesus Christ.

Revelation 5:10

> *"And have made us kings and priests to our God; and we shall reign on the earth."*

This is the final outcome of the Lord's work, death and ressurection. We will come back to this earth with Christ to rule and reign with Him as priests and kings.

Revelation 5:11&12

> *"Then I looked, and I heard the voice of many angels around the throne, the living creatures, and the elders; and the number of them was ten thousand times ten thousand, and thousands of thousands, saying with a loud voice: "Worthy is the Lamb who was slain to receive power and riches and wisdom, and strength and honor and glory and blessing!"*

Try and visualize what this scene must have looked like to John. Up to this point his focus was on the splendor of the throne. Now he is starting to focus on other things going on around him. He is in awe by the innumerable angels, thousands upon thousands all around him, all worshipping and praising Jesus at the same time in total harmony.

Revelation 5:13

> *"And every creature which is in heaven and on the earth and under the earth and such as are in the sea, and all that are in them, I heard saying: "Blessing and honor and glory and power be to Him who sits on the throne, and to the Lamb, forever and ever!"*

John is overwhelmed by everything he is seeing and hearing around him (as I imagine will happen to each and every one of us when we are in the presence of God). The sound must be astonishing for him to hear every creature in the universe singing their praises to the Lord at the same time in perfect harmony.

Revelation 5:14

> *"Then the four living creatures said, "Amen!" And the twenty-four elders fell down and worshipped Him who lives forever and ever."*

When the four beasts say amen, the entire redeemed church represented by the twenty-four elders fall down and worship Jesus. I can't wait to be in front of the throne of Almighty God with John and everyone else, praising and worshipping our King.

CHAPTER 6

Revelation 6:1

> *"Now I saw when the Lamb opened one of the seals; and I heard one of the four living creatures saying with a voice like thunder, "Come and see."*

It is the Lamb who was sacrificed for our sins opening the seals and is worthy, but it will be the Lion who comes back to mete out judgment. Thunder and lightning in scripture represent judgment and power of Almighty God.

One of the four beasts summons John to come and look at what is about to happen on the earth.

Revelation 6:2a

> *"And I looked, and behold, a white horse. And he who sat on it had a bow; and a crown was given to him."*

The white horse symbolizes a conqueror, conquest, battles, war and victory.

The rider, symbolic of the antichrist has a bow but no arrows. He will cause a war so he can establish temporary world peace. He will seem to have the perfect plan to solve all the world's problems. Even the Israeli and Arab nations will be fooled by him and sign a seven year peace treaty marking the start of the Great Tribulation. He will be eloquent in speech and have a brilliant mind especially in politics, war and understanding today's troubles.

This will fulfill the scriptures:
> "He will confirm a covenant with many for one seven (year period). In the middle of the seven (3½ years) he will put an end to sacrifice and offering. And on a wing of the temple, he will set up an abomination that causes desolation, until the end that is decreed is poured out on him." (Daniel 9:27) (NIV)

[SEE ALSO: DANIEL 7:8B; 8:23-25; 11:36-38]

He is given the victor's crown. In Greek it is called the "stephanos", which was given to anyone who was victorious in war, yet his final demise is set and nothing can change it.

Revelation 6:2b

> "And he went out conquering and to conquer."

The antichrist will try to imitate Christ as the messiah of Israel and will conquer the world through a false peace and a false religion that will sound pleasing and acceptable to everyone.

Revelation 6:3&4

> "When He had opened the second seal, I heard the second living creature saying, "Come and see." And another horse, fiery red, went out. And it was granted to the one who sat on it to take peace from the earth, and that people should kill one another; and there was given to him a great sword."

The red horse symbolizes blood representing war and conflict. As in Revelation 6:1&2, it is Christ who gives the power to the riders of the horses. Satan is in the process of trying to bring the world together through a false peace. Some nations will realize (a little late) what the antichrist is trying to do and will revolt causing a major world war to break out. Scripture reveals to us that the attempt to overthrow the antichrist will fail.

It is evident from the opening of the next two seals that this will be a bloody and devastating war.

Revelation 6:4c

"And that people should kill one another;"

This indicates violence and savagery. Many will be at war and death will be overwhelming. The war will cause a shortage of almost everything and people will start killing each other to pillage for supplies.

Revelation 6:4c

"And there was given to him a great sword."

This is a symbol of great power and authority. It illustrates what heaven authorizes, earth executes.

There are two different words for sword used in the Bible. The sword of a soldier who goes marching into war is "rhomphaia" and means a long sword or saber.

In the above verse the word is "machaira" which is a short jagged dagger that usually was hidden under the coat, and was known as "the assassin's weapon". It was widely used to slit the throat of an animal or a man. In today's world, we can see all these things taking place, but this is just a foreshadowing of what is yet to come. Jesus told His disciples:

> *"And you will hear of wars and rumors of wars. See that you are not troubled; for all these things must come to pass, but the end is not yet. For nation will rise against nation, and kingdom against kingdom. And there will be famines, pestilences, and earthquakes in various places. All these are the beginning of sorrows." (Matthew 24:6-8)*

I believe this is the time we are living in now, the beginning of sorrows.

Revelation 6:5&6

> "When He opened the third seal, I heard the third living creature say, "Come and see." And I looked, and behold, a black horse, and he who sat on it had a pair of scales in his hand. And I heard a voice in the midst of the four living creatures saying, "A quart of wheat for a denarius (penny), and three quarts of barley for a denarius (penny); and do not harm the oil and the wine."

The black horse symbolizes famine which is a natural result of war. There will be a lack of men to till the soil and harvest the crops. Black is used throughout scriptures to depict famine.

> "I looked up again – and there before me were four chariots coming out from between two mountains – mountains of bronze! The first chariot had red horses, the second black, the third white and the fourth dappled (spotted) – all of them powerful. I asked the angel who was speaking to me, 'What are these, my lord?' The angel answered me, 'These are the four spirits of heaven, going out from standing in the presence of the LORD of the whole world. The one with the black horses is going toward the North Country, one with the white horses toward the west, and the one with the dappled horses go forth toward the south. When the powerful horses went out, they were straining to go throughout the earth. And he said, 'Go throughout the earth!' So they went throughout the earth." (Zechariah 6:1-7) (NIV)

A shortage of food always drives up prices and forces the governments to ration what is available. The pair of scales in the hand of the rider indicates the scarcity of food in the end times. Ezekiel 4:16 & Leviticus 26:26 both indicates when bread has to be weighed and portioned out it is a condition of severe famine.

A denarius (penny) is the Biblical reference to the equivalent of a man's wages for a day's work. In the end times food will be so scarce that it will cost a day's wages just to buy a loaf of bread.

A measure of wheat is about 1 quart, and 3 measures of barley is about a pint. It is a minimum daily sustenance diet, just enough to keep a person barely alive. This will be the daily ration of food allowed per person in the end times.

Revelation 6:6c

> "And do not harm the oil and the wine."

Oil and wine were considered the rich man's luxuries in biblical times. Rich people generally will not be as affected by the famine as the poor or middle class people. The oil they mention here is the oil that comes from olives. Olives and olive oil is one of the main crops of the mid-east. The grapes and olives are spared destruction.

Today more than half of the world (3.5 billion) goes to bed hungry every night. At least 10,000 people die of malnutrition every day. The garbage from one home in the United States would feed a family of six each day in India. The average American dog has a higher protein diet than many people of the world.

Revelation 6:7&8

> "When He opened the fourth seal, I heard the voice of the fourth living creature saying, "Come and see." And I looked, and behold, a pale horse. And the name of him who sat on it was Death, and Hades followed with him. And power was given to them over a fourth of the earth, to kill with sword, with hunger, with death, and by the beasts of the earth."

The Greek word for pale is translated "chloros" (khlo-ros) which means: greenish, verdant, dun- colored or green.

Unlike the other three riders this rider has a name - Death. Hades is the realm of the unsaved dead. One quarter of the earth's population will be wiped out by these four horsemen. That would be over 1.5 Billion people which is six times the current population of the United States.

God gives us life, and it is God who has the right to take it away. He is giving authority to the four horsemen to do His wrath upon the earth.

Death has weapons with him.

"War" – The antichrist's army will fight the nations of the world to establish his false peace.

"Hunger"- Famine always follows war and people get desperate when they are hungry and will go to any extreme to get food.

> "You shall eat the fruit of your own body, the flesh of your sons and your daughters whom the LORD your God has given you, in the siege and desperate straits in which your enemy shall distress you." (Deuteronomy 28:53)

[SEE ALSO: LEVITICUS 26:27-29; ISAIAH 9:20; JEREMIAH 19:9]

"Pestilence and disease" - With hunger and starvation always follows disease, filth and pestilence (rodents).

"Death" - Death itself is used as a weapon here. The word death is translated "thanatoo" (than-at-o-o) which means to kill, or (cause to be) put to death.

"Beasts of the earth" - The word beast in this verse in Greek is "therion" (thay-ree-on) meaning a dangerous animal, venomous, a wild beast and a wild animal as game.

When there is famine, starvation and pestilence among people, it will also be among the animals. A hungry animal gets vicious (rabid) and will kill whatever it can for food including people, especially babies and small children.

> These weapons are described as four sore judgments to fall upon Jerusalem: *"For thus says the Lord God: How much more it shall be when I send My four severe judgments on Jerusalem - the sword and famine and wild beasts and pestilence - to cut off man and beast from it?"* (Ezekiel 14:21)

Revelation 6:9-10

"When He opened the fifth seal, I saw under the altar the souls of those who had been slain for the word of God and for the testimony which they held. And they cried with a loud voice, saying, "How long, O Lord, holy and true, until You judge and avenge our blood on those who dwell on the earth?"

John does not see or mention the souls under the altar until after the fifth seal is opened. The seals are judgments for those who do not follow Jesus and for the cleansing of the Jews.

We know from Revelation 5:8-10 that these souls under the altar cannot be *"the church"* because the church has already been raptured (I Thessalonians 4:13-18 and I Corinthians 15:51-58). These souls under the altar are the tribulation saints and martyrs that were slaughtered by the antichrist, the beast and the false prophet for not accepting the mark of the beast (666), or bowing to the image of the beast.

[SEE ALSO: REVELATION 20:4]

These souls are under the altar of incense (*Revelation 8:5; 9:13*) nearest to God, which is the place where God receives fragrant aromas. The sacrifice is pleasing to God. The testimony they held is the testimony of the gospel.

Once the church is called to heaven the period of being *saved by grace* comes to an end. To be saved during the tribulation will mean being martyred.

The fact that the souls: *"cried out with a loud voice saying "How long, O Lord, holy and true, dost Thou not judge and avenge our blood"* shows these souls can speak, have feelings, thoughts and can hear. They are crying to God to *judge and avenge* which is proof that these are not the church saints. In the tribulation, God will be delivering judgment and the cry of the new believers for revenge will be justified.

Revelation 6:11

> *"And a white robe was given to each of them; and it was said to them, that they should rest a little while longer, until both the number of their fellow servants and their brethren, who would be killed as they were, was completed."*

The white robes reveal these souls from the great tribulation were martyred for their testimony of Jesus Christ, not denying Jesus and not bowing to the antichrist. White garments are the proper attire for those in the presence of God.

They are told to *"rest yet for a "little season" until their "fellow servants"* (*"sundoulos"* [soon-doo-los]; *a servitor or ministrant of the same master, [human or divine]), and their "brethren" ("adelphos" [ad-el-fos]; the womb, a brother [literally or figuratively]), that should be killed as they were, should be fulfilled"*. God clearly has a set number of those who will be killed during this period. There are two particular periods mentioned in Revelation when the Jews will be heavily martyred. The first time is under the fifth seal and later in Revelation 7:9 the greatest slaughter of believers the world has ever seen will take place.

Revelation 6:12

> *"I looked when He opened the sixth seal and behold, there was a great earthquake; and the sun became black as sackcloth of hair, and the moon became like blood."*

The opening of the sixth seal takes place at the half way mark of the seven year Great Tribulation and ushers in the last three and a half years. When the sixth seal is opened the wrath of God will be revealed. The wrath of God is not revealed in the first five seals because things happen naturally from the rise of the antichrist to power.

The antichrist has been butchering the martyrs for the first three and a half years as he seduced the nations of the world to follow him. Now he breaks his peace treaty with Israel and goes to war against Israel for the last three and a half years.

God takes His vengeance out on all those who follow the antichrist, worship the beast and accept his mark (666). An earthquake occurs that is so devastating that every mountain and island will be *"moved out of their places"*. Yet as terrible as this earthquake will be it will dim in comparison to the earthquake yet to come. Still people do not repent after this devastating earthquake that will shake the very foundations of the earth.

The people will know this is God's wrath falling on them because of their disobedience but they do not ask forgiveness. Instead, they ask the rocks and mountains to hide them. Their hearts are so hard, their minds so evil and their bodies so full of sin they try to hide from God rather than acknowledge and turn to Him.

There are several reasons for the sun turning black as a sackcloth of hair. The sun does not actually turn black, but the devastation taking place on earth at this time causes it to appear black. The earthquake is so tremendous that the dust from the collapse of millions of buildings, structures, roads and bridges, added to the dirt and rubble of the mountains collapsing and avalanches and islands shifting that the sun will be blocked out. In 1970, 67,000 lives were lost in one devastating earthquake and in the last 4,000 years over thirteen million lives were lost to earthquakes.

In December of 2004, over 100,000 lives were lost and 5,000,000 people became homeless in a matter of minutes because of an earthquake in the depths of the ocean that caused a giant tsunami (tidal wave) to hit several countries at once and cover entire islands. In 2009, Haiti was leveled by a massive earthquake, and in 2011 Japan was struck by the largest earthquake ever recorded, a 9.0 which also caused a massive tsunami to strike Japan with 35 foot waves destroying three nuclear reactors then reaching the shores of Hawaii and the west coast of the United States. The above mentioned earthquake disasters will pale in comparison to what will happen at the opening of the sixth seal. Such a catastrophic earthquake will cause volcanoes to erupt.

On different occasions throughout history volcanic eruptions threw ash miles into the atmosphere which blackened the sun for days. Because the sun was so darkened from the ash, the moon looked like blood.

On August 27th, 1883 a volcano that erupted in Krakatau, East Indies was heard erupting in Rodriguez, South America, three thousand miles away. The sun was blotted out from this volcano at Batavia, located 100 miles away and at Bonduel, 150 miles away. The sun blotted out the moon and appeared blood red while a tidal wave hit Cape Horn, 7,000 miles away and killed 36,000 people.

As bad as the above volcanic eruption sounds, it will also pale in comparison to what will happen during the great tribulation.

Revelation 6:13

> *"And the stars of heaven fell to the earth, as a fig tree drops its late figs when it is shaken by a mighty wind."*

Thousands of meteors will fall to the earth but instead of being burned up as they enter the atmosphere, some of them will impact the earth weighing thousands of pounds. Normally they are the size of a grain of sand, or a small pebble. On November 13th, 1833 shooting stars fell continuously for three hours. The people at that time thought the world was coming to an end.

Visualize a pitch black sky caused by all heavenly light blocked out by the earthquake and the volcanoes. All electricity will be knocked out and suddenly thousands upon thousands of shooting stars, bigger and more brilliant than you have ever seen will streak through the darkness, breaking through the atmosphere and smashing into the earth. Not only will everything in their path be destroyed, but they will hit with such force that the foundation of the earth will be shaken.

Revelation 6:14

> *"Then the sky receded as a scroll when it is rolled up, and every mountain and island was moved out of its place."*

Because of the combination of the earthquake, volcanoes and stars falling to the earth shaking the planet, heaven itself will be affected. The clouds and the sky will no longer be blue and white, but will roll up together like a scroll of ancient parchment.

[SEE ALSO: ISAIAH 34:4&5]

Revelation 6:15&16

> "And the kings of the earth, the great men, the rich men, the commanders, the mighty men, every slave and every free man, hid themselves in the caves and in the rocks of the mountains, and said to the mountains and rocks, "Fall on us and hide us from the face of Him who sits on the throne and from the wrath of the Lamb!"

This is God's judgment. When the heavens roll up as a scroll, the people on earth will know it is the wrath of God. They try to hide from God in caves and dens of the mountains and will ask the rocks and mountains to fall on them. They will talk to rocks but they won't talk to God. How foolish they would rather die than repent.

Revelation 6:17

> "For the great day of His wrath has come, and who is able to stand?"

The earth will shake so violently it will move off its axis and possibly shift its orbit. We had a very small taste of that happening from the power of the earthquake that caused the giant tsunami in December of 2004. Scientists said that the earth shifted "1,000,000 of 1 degree". January 12th, 2010 the 7.0 earthquake which struck Haiti shifted earth once again "1,000,000 of 1 degree".
[SEE ALSO: ISAIAH 13:6-13]

Eventually the unbelievers will try to make war with Christ because Satan will have them deceived into believing they can destroy God.

CHAPTER 7

Revelation 7:1a

"After these things"

What things? Everything John has already seen - the opening of the first six seals. John will now be shown the next set of events to take place.

Revelation 7:1b

"I saw four angels standing at the four corners of the earth, holding the four winds of the earth, that the wind should not blow on the earth, on the sea, or on any tree."

There will not be the slightest breeze anywhere in the world.

Revelation 7:2&3

"Then I saw another angel ascending from the east, having the seal of the living God. And he cried with a loud voice to the four angels to whom it was granted to harm the earth and the sea, saying, "Do not harm the earth, the sea, or the trees till we have sealed the servants of our God on their foreheads."

An angel rises out of the east and commands the four angels *"not to hurt the earth, sea or trees"* until the servants of God are sealed. This seal is visible to God, the angels, the antichrist, beast and false prophet. Whether the seal will be visible to the human eye is unclear. This is not the first time the Lord had someone marked with a seal. In Genesis, the LORD set a mark upon Cain which was visible to everyone (Genesis 4:15). In Ezekiel 9:4 the LORD ordered "A mark upon the foreheads of the men that sigh and that cry for all the abominations that be done in the midst thereof." From reading these scriptures, I believe the mark will be visible to everyone during the tribulation.

Revelation 7:4

> "And I heard the number of those who were sealed. One hundred and forty-four thousand of all the tribes of the children of Israel were sealed."

This is a seal to distinguish the 144,000 chosen Israelites of the original 12 tribes of Israel from everybody else that is on the earth at this time. These people are from the original blood line families of Israelites who are named by their tribes.

Revelation 7:5-8

> "of the tribe of Judah twelve thousand were sealed;
> of the tribe of Reuben twelve thousand were sealed;
> of the tribe of Gad twelve thousand were sealed;
> of the tribe of Asher twelve thousand were sealed;
> of the tribe of Naphtali twelve thousand were sealed;
> of the tribe of Manasseh twelve thousand were sealed.
> of the tribe of Simeon twelve thousand were sealed;
> of the tribe of Levi twelve thousand were sealed;
> of the tribe of Issachar twelve thousand were sealed;
> of the tribe of Zebulun twelve thousand were sealed;
> of the tribe of Joseph twelve thousand were sealed;
> of the tribe of Benjamin twelve thousand were sealed."

> *These 144,000 will not be hurt during the tribulation by the plagues, wrath of God, the antichrist, the beast or false prophet. Just as God protected Israel in the Old Testament when He sent the different plagues and pestilence throughout Egypt so Pharaoh would let the Israelites leave the land, He will also protect them now in these end time plagues (Exodus 7-12).*

Revelation 7:9&10

> *"After these things I looked, and behold, a great multitude which no one could number, of all nations, tribes, peoples, and tongues, standing before the throne and before the Lamb, clothed with white robes, with palm branches in their hands, and crying out with a loud voice, saying, "Salvation belongs to our God who sits on the throne, and to the Lamb!"*

After the twelve tribes are sealed John witnesses *"a great multitude, which no man could number, of all nations, tribes, peoples and tongues, stand before the throne, and before the Lamb, clothed in white robes"*. Notice that he doesn't say, from all "religions" or "denominations" but all who profess Christ. Only believers in Jesus Christ as the Son of God will stand before the throne of God in the first resurrection.

During this period the greatest revival in the history of the world will probably take place. These 144,000 Israelites will be filled with the Holy Spirit and have the full knowledge of the scriptures. They will be able to show people through the scriptures why millions of people suddenly disappeared.

After Christ ascended into heaven, His apostles went throughout the world proclaiming the gospel between 33A.D. and 98A.D. They converted hundreds of thousands of Jews and gentiles to Christianity. Can you imagine what 144,000 will be able to do in today's population with another out pouring of the Holy Spirit like there was at the day of Pentecost?

The sun did not go black nor did the moon turn to blood at Pentecost when Peter preached *(Acts 2:16-18)*, so this event which the prophet Joel wrote about *(Joel 2:28&29)* and the apostle Peter preached about is still a future event.

This *"great multitude that no man could number"* is not the raptured church, because the church has white robes with the *"victor crowns"* *(Revelation4:4)*. These have white robes and *"palm branches"*. The white robes show they are redeemed from the earth, while the palm branches indicate rejoicing and victory in Christ. When Christ rode into Jerusalem on the donkey, the people waved palm branches, singing *"hosanna"* which means (oh save!), and praised Jesus as the King of Israel.

[SEE ALSO: MATTHEW 21:7-9; MARK 11:9&10]

They are crying with loud voices saying *"Salvation to our God which sits on the throne and unto the Lamb"*, which reveals these redeemed Jews and Gentiles are the recipients of personal salvation. Nothing is going to stop them from singing, praising and worshipping God.

Jesus tells us that the angels of heaven rejoice when just one sinner comes to repentance *Luke 15:7&10*.

Revelation 7:11&12

> *"And all the angels stood around the throne and the elders and the four living creatures, and fell on their faces before the throne and worshipped God,*

> *Saying: "Amen! Blessing and glory and wisdom*
> *Thanksgiving and honor and power and might,*
> *Be unto our God for ever and ever. Amen."*

What it will sound like in heaven at this moment when the praise of all the angels joins with the praise of all the redeemed? The angels open and close this praise with *Amen* which means "so be it."

Revelation 7:13&14

> *"Then one of the elders answered, saying to me, "Who are these arrayed in white robes, and where did they come from?" And I said to him, "Sir, you know." So he said to me, "These are the ones who come out of the great tribulation, and washed their robes and made them white in the blood of the Lamb."*

The elder asks John two very specific questions:

1. Who are these people arrayed in white robes?
2. Where did they come from?

John is baffled and says to the elder *"I don't know who they are, but I know that you know."*

The elder answers his own question. He tells John: *"these are they which came out of great tribulation"*. These tribulation saints are a distinct group just as the New Testament church, the Old Testament saints, Israel and the Jews are all distinct groups. Each group has its own type of relationship to God and to the Lamb. That these are believers is unquestionable because they have *"washed their robes and made them white in the blood of the Lamb"*. They are before the throne of God which makes it clear that they have just as many eternal blessings as the believers of the other groups.

Revelation 7:15-17

> "Therefore they are before the throne of God, and serve Him day and night in His temple. And He who sits on the throne will dwell among them. They shall neither hunger anymore nor thirst anymore; the sun shall not strike them, nor any heat; For the Lamb who is in the midst of the throne will shepherd them and lead them to living fountains of waters. And God will wipe away every tear from their eyes."

These saints will be martyred throughout the great tribulation. We have seen that the *"souls under the altar"* will have been slain from the time of the rapture of the church till the end of the great tribulation period. Those who will be faithful unto death during this time will serve God in His temple forever. Revelation 7:17 reveals that the Lamb (Jesus), will feed them from now on and lead them to living waters which scripture tells us comes from the midst of the throne of God and of the Lamb.

Revelation 7:17b

> "God shall wipe away all tears from their eyes."

This verse is still in the future.

Revelation 21:1-7 Clarifies the *"wiping away of all tears"* does not happen until after the white throne judgment. This particular group of tribulation martyrs receives a special blessing. They are specifically chosen to serve day and night forevermore before the throne and God will dwell among them. They will never hunger or thirst again and because they will forever be in the presence of Almighty God, they will have no need for the sun or its heat, for God is their light.

CHAPTER 8

Revelation 8:1

> "When He opened the seventh seal, there was silence in heaven for about half an hour."

In the previous chapters there were angels singing, Old Testament, New Testament and martyred tribulation saints rejoicing, worshipping and praising God in heaven. On earth there was devastation, thunder, lightning, volcanic eruptions and earthquakes of enormous magnitude. Now there is silence so loud it's deafening. Like the ultimate calm before the storm there is complete silence throughout the heavens. There is neither a bird chirping nor the sound of the slightest breeze blowing. No angels are singing and no saints are worshipping. To the inhabitants of the earth this will be terrifying.

God in His ultimate love and compassion for the human race (*not willing that any should perish, but that all should come to repentance (II Peter 3:9)* is giving a half hour for the people on earth to contemplate all that they have seen and heard and to repent and turn to Him before He unleashes the full power of His wrath.

Revelation 8:2

> "And I saw the seven angels who stand before God and to them were given seven trumpets."

The seven angels are each given a trumpet. Trumpets were used in scripture to warn of impending trouble or danger. Trumpets were also used for rejoicing and solemn occasions when they were blown over the burnt offerings and fellowship offerings as a memorial to the people before God.

[SEE ALSO: NUMBERS 10:8-10]

For the inhabitants of earth these seven trumpets are warnings of judgment and doom but for the tribulation martyrs the trumpets are for rejoicing because God is about to avenge His people and answer the prayers of the *"souls under the altar"* (Revelation 6:9).

Revelation 8:3-5

"Then another angel, having a golden censer, came and stood at the altar. And he was given much incense that he should offer it with the prayers of all saints upon the golden altar which was before the throne. And the smoke of the incense, with the prayers of the saints, ascended before God from the angel's hand. Then the angel took the censer, filled it with fire from the altar, and threw it to the earth. And there were noises, thundering, lightning, and an earthquake."

Scripture reveals this angel priest is Jesus. Only Jesus has the right and the authority to offer up our prayers to His Father. Jesus is the only mediator between God and man *(1 Timothy 2:5)*. Jesus is the only one who died for us.

In the Old Testament Jesus is often referred to as the "Angel of the LORD" *(Judges 2:1&4)*.

The altar on which incense is burned in the Old Testament was set up in the tent of the congregation just before the door (veil) of the tabernacle where the Ark of the Covenant was kept.

[SEE ALSO: EXODUS 30:6]

Aaron (the high priest) burned the incense on the altar. Once a year he made an atonement upon the horns of the altar with the *"blood of the sin offering"*, which is *"most holy unto the LORD"*. Only the high priest could make this atonement with blood and only the high priest could burn the sweet smelling incense on the altar. The censer is always mentioned in connection with the high priest.
[SEE ALSO: LEVITICUS 16:12&13]

When the censer is thrown, the silence in the heavens and the earth are shattered. In Revelation 5:8 just before Jesus opened the seven seals, the elders and cherubim had *"golden bowls full of incense, which are the prayers of saints"*. In both instances it was the prayers of the saints which preceded and initiated the opening of the seals and the blowing of the trumpets.

Revelation 8:7

> *"The first angel sounded: And hail and fire followed, mingled with blood, and they were thrown to the earth; and a third of the trees were burned up, and all green grass was burned up."*

The aftermath of the first angel blowing his trumpet is one third of all the trees and all the grass are burned up. The LORD placed a similar judgment upon the land of Egypt when Pharaoh refused to let Moses and the Israelites leave *(Exodus 9:24-26)*. The prayers *ascended*; judgment *descended*.

Think of the ecological impact this judgment will have on the earth. Imagine all the smoke, ash, heat and pollution. The clean air is destroyed; the oxygen is used up by the fire to support the burning and people and animals will suffocate and die from this first of seven trumpet judgments.

Revelation 8:8&9

> "Then the second angel sounded: And something like a great mountain burning with fire was thrown into the sea and a third of the sea became blood; and a third of the living creatures in the sea died, and a third of the ships were destroyed."

There will be a terrible stench from the creatures in the seas and oceans dying and washing up on the shores. Add one third of all the ships being destroyed leaving rotting flesh from dead bodies and the result will be ugly and disgusting in appearance and smell. The pollution will be devastating.

According to the IMO (International Maritime Organization) as of 2011 there are more than 159,442 ocean going merchant ships and 103,392 commercial ships registered around the world in more than 150 countries. Imagine what approximately 87,611 ships being destroyed simultaneously will do to the shipping industry and the economy. How many other jobs will be affected? It's beyond imagination and there are five trumpets yet to sound.

Revelation 8:10&11

> "Then the third angel sounded: And a great star fell from heaven, burning like a torch, and it fell on a third of the rivers and on the springs of water; and the name of the star is Wormwood; and a third of the waters became wormwood; and many men died from the water, because it was made bitter."

This star or meteor will hit the fresh water supply of the earth poisoning one third of the fresh water on the earth. Many people will die from drinking this water and using it in their food.

The Greek word for "wormwood" is *(apsinthos)* and means bitterness. In the Hebrew language it is *(la'anah)* and means cursed, poisonous, and accursed.

National Geographic lists approximately 100 principal rivers in the world ranging in length from 4,000 miles long (the Amazon River) to the (Rio De La Plata River) which is 150 miles long. The U.S. Geological survey reports 30 large rivers in the United States beginning with the Mississippi which is 3,710 miles long.

Revelation 8:12

> "Then the fourth angel sounded: and a third of the sun was struck, a third of the moon, and a third of the stars, so that a third of them were darkened; and a third of the day did not shine, and likewise the night."

When the fourth angel blows his trumpet, we will go from a 24 hour day to a 16 hour day. Even though this is a punishment to the unbelievers of the earth, it is also necessary for the survival of God's elect (the Jews and the martyrs) who are still on the earth. No one would survive the intense heat during the day and extreme cold during the night if this did not happen.

[SEE ALSO: AMOS 8:9; MATTHEW 24:21&22]

Revelation 8:13

> "And I looked, and I heard an angel flying through the midst of heaven, saying with a loud voice, "Woe, woe, woe, to the inhabitants of the earth, because of the remaining blasts of the trumpet of the three angels who are about to sound!"

Before the fifth angel sounds his trumpet, God in His mercy and love for mankind is still giving the inhabitants of the earth a chance to repent. He sends an angel to fly throughout the earth to give a warning that what already has happened on the earth is nothing in comparison to what is about to happen. Scripture states no one will have an excuse in end times to say they didn't know the message of the gospel.

[SEE ALSO: MATTHEW 24:14; REVELATION 14:6&7]

Whenever you see the word *Woe* in the Scriptures – Look Out, there is big trouble about to take place. You will want to be as far away as possible from what is about to happen. Where there is a woe in scripture, death and destruction follow.

CHAPTER 9

Revelation 9:1&2

> "Then the fifth angel sounded: and I saw a star fall from heaven to the earth. And to him was given the key to the bottomless pit. And he opened the bottomless pit, and smoke arose out of the pit like the smoke of a great furnace. And the sun and the air were darkened because of the smoke of the pit."

The star John sees falling is not an actual star, but rather an angel from heaven. The word star is used in scripture several times to denote angels.
[SEE ALSO: JUDGES 5:20; JUDE 13B]

   The fallen angels that followed Satan are also referred to as stars. (*Revelation 12:4*)

   This angel that opens the pit also appears in *Revelation 20:1-3*. This cannot be a fallen angel because he certainly wouldn't try to bind his king (Satan) and cast him in the bottomless pit. Scriptures reveal that this angel is none other than Michael the Archangel. Whenever battles or wars are taking place between good and bad angels, Michael is always there.
[SEE ALSO: DANIEL 10:13&21; JUDE 9]

   Michael the Archangel opens the bottomless pit and John sees smoke so thick it darkens the sun and pollutes the air we breathe. People will be choking, gasping for fresh air. Their eyes will burn and people will die from suffocation.

Revelation 9:3-11

> "Then out of the smoke locusts came upon the earth. And to them was given power, as the scorpions of the earth have power. They were commanded not to harm the grass of the earth, or any green thing, or any tree, but only those men who do not have the seal of God on their foreheads. And they were not given authority to kill them, but to torment them for five months. And their torment was like the torment of a scorpion when it strikes a man. In those days men will seek death and will not find it; they will desire to die, and death will flee from them. And the shape of the locusts was like horses prepared for battle; and on their heads were crowns of something like gold, and their faces were like the faces of men. They had hair like women's hair, and their teeth were like lions' teeth. And they had breastplates like breastplates of iron, and the sound of their wings was like the sound of chariots with many horses running into battle. They had tails like scorpions, and there were stings in their tails. And their power was to hurt men five months. And they had as king over them the angel of the bottomless pit, whose name in Hebrew is Abaddon, but in Greek he has the name Apollyon"

I have never seen a swarm of locusts except on television and they looked like a thick black cloud dark enough to block out the sun light.

Ordinary locusts are considered clean food for eating and have been for centuries (Leviticus 11:22). These locusts are not ordinary plant eating locusts and are unlike locusts mentioned anywhere else in the Bible. They are intelligent beings. Revelation 9:4 says: "it was commanded them". These demon locusts have the ability to think and obey commands and are told to leave the grass and trees and herbs alone.

They are given power like a scorpion. Scorpions sting with their tail and their poison is deadly to most animals but not usually potent enough to kill a human being although it will make them violently ill and cause excruciating pain. These locusts are also commanded to only hurt those men who do not have the seal of God.

These locusts will stay around for five months and *Revelation 9:5* says they will not kill, but anyone who gets stung by them will be tormented. *Revelation 9:7* says that the shape of the locusts were *"like horses prepared unto battle."* If you closely examine a locust, you will see that they almost look like tiny horses. Revelation 9:7b says that *"On their heads were crowns like gold."* These demon locusts seem to be wearing victory (stephanos) crowns. Nothing can destroy them until their mission is accomplished.

The prophet Joel gave a distinct similarity of Revelation 9:7. Joel prophesied almost 2,500 years ahead of time about the fifth trumpet on The LORD'S Day (*Joel 2:1-10*). Joel's description is not of literal horses. Horses do not climb walls, climb up roofs or enter windows like a thief. Horses do not fly in the heavens nor in such numbers as to darken the sun, moon and stars, and they certainly do not escape being wounded if pierced in battle, but demon locust can.

Revelation 9:8

"They had hair like women's hair"

During the time John wrote this book there was nothing considered more seductive about a woman than her hair. Though these locusts are repulsive creatures they seem to have an intriguing almost seductive nature which will stir the curiosity of man. They have teeth like lions which seem to be a defensive weapon, since their power to make man sick is in their tails. Their *"breast plates like iron"* help make them indestructible from the weapons of mankind. They are impressive creatures: *"the sound of their wings is as the sound of chariots of many horses running to battle"*.

Have you ever come close to stepping on a grasshopper and hear how loud it is when it tries to get out of your way? Imagine what millions of these demon locusts will sound like with their wings beating as they fly?

An angel from the bottomless pit is king over the demon locusts. That Scripture revealed his name means he must be a very important or powerful Angel. Even though Scriptures say there are *"ten thousand times ten thousand times thousand and thousands of angels"* (Revelation 5:11), the Scriptures only name a few of them: Michael the archangel, Gabriel and Lucifer (Satan). This angel's name in the Hebrew tongue is "Abaddon" which means green, like a locust.

Revelation 9:12-16

> *"One woe is past. Behold, still two more woes are coming after these things."*
>
> *"Then the sixth angel sounded: And I heard a voice from the four horns of the golden altar which is before God, saying to the sixth angel who had the trumpet, "Release the four angels who are bound at the great river Euphrates. So the four angels, who had been prepared for the hour and day and month and year, were released to kill a third of mankind. Now the number of the army of the horsemen was two hundred million, and I heard the number of them."*

John is again standing at the golden altar before God. A voice speaks from the four horns of the altar telling the sixth angel to loose the four angels bound in the Euphrates River. These are fallen angels. There is no reason God would have any of His heavenly angels bound. These angels are very destructive and evil since they had to be bound so they could not cause a problem or act sooner than God wanted them to. These angels were prepared for this specific moment in time to slay a third of mankind.

In *Revelation 6:1-8* we read one fourth of mankind was killed by the four horsemen of the apocalypse. Now, one third of all mankind that was left will be killed by the army led by these four angels from the Euphrates.

In the first woe the demon locusts caused great pain to mankind, but no one died. In this second woe these demons will cause the death and destruction of mankind.

Some people mistake this for *Armageddon*, but this is not the armies of the world gathered against Israel. This is a demon army. John hears the size of the army - it is two hundred thousand times a thousand, which equals: 200,000,000 horse like creatures with riders directing them.

Revelation 9:17-19

> *"And thus I saw the horses in the vision: and those who sat on them had breastplates of fiery red, hyacinth blue, and sulfur yellow; and the heads of the horses were like the heads of lions; and out of their mouths came fire, smoke, and brimstone. By these three plagues a third of mankind was killed-by the fire and the smoke and the brimstone which came out of their mouths. For their power is in their mouth and in their tails; for their tails are like serpents, having heads; and with them they do harm."*

John knows what horses look like. He recognizes immediately that these are not normal horses. The heads are shaped like lions and out of their mouths come fire, smoke and brimstone. Some people believe that John is trying to describe modern day military weapons. If this was the case, he would have described them as some form of beast he had no name for, but he doesn't. He says they are horses that have the heads of lions with power in their tails shaped like serpents which can do harm.

The "four horsemen of the apocalypse" destroyed one fourth of the world population and this demon army will destroy another one third which means that approximately 3.5 billion of the world's present day population will be dead. Since the population of the world grows every year, the tally could far exceed the 3.5 billion by the time the seven year great tribulation begins.

One half of the world's population is now dead!

Revelation 9:20

> "But the rest of mankind, who were not killed by these plagues, did not repent of the works of their hands, that they should not worship demons, and idols of gold, silver, brass, stone, and wood, which can neither see nor hear nor walk;"

Though these are demons with a demon king leading them, they are still under the authority of Almighty God. The *"works of their hands"* are what man makes from gold, silver, brass, stone, wood and any other material possible and then worships as god. These are objects; unlike Jesus who is our living God.
[SEE ALSO: HEBREWS 9:14]

The Lord is warning us against devil worship. Some people are naive enough to think demons don't exist. Others think it's just harmless fun to mess with such things as Ouija boards, séances and fortune tellers but God warns us through Scripture not to get involved with such things lest we open the door for spiritual attack. [SEE ALSO: 1 SAMUEL 28:7-15]

Revelation 9:21

> "And they did not repent of their murders, or their sorceries or their sexual immorality or their thefts."

People still have not learned their lesson. Besides worshipping false idols, they still murder, steal, commit adultery, participate in homosexuality, incest and engage in sorceries. The Greek word for sorceries is "pharmakeia" *(far-mak-i-ah)* which means: medication, pharmacy, magic and witchcraft. God is giving man every chance to repent, but because of the hardness of their hearts, even after the two woes which have taken place, they still refuse.

CHAPTER 10

Revelation 10 through *Revelation 11:14* is an interlude between the sixth and seventh trumpet. John is describing an event that takes place after the sixth trumpet sounds but before the seventh trumpet. It is similar to a digression during a story that is necessary to fully understand the ending of the story. John is filling in some important details before he continues to the seventh trumpet so you will better understand what is happening.

Revelation 10:1

> *"And I saw still another mighty angel coming down from heaven, clothed with a cloud. And a rainbow was on His head, His face was like the sun, and His feet like pillars of fire."*

These chapters of Revelation are dealing with Israel so it is not surprising Jesus is being called *The Angel of the LORD*, the name that Israel is familiar with throughout their history. Jesus is the only one in the Bible described as being *"clothed with a cloud, a rainbow on his head, his face shinning as the sun, and his feet a pillar of fire."*

Sometimes Jesus appeared as a man, such as when He appeared to Abraham as *Melchizedek King of Salem*. *"Then Melchizedek king of Salem brought out bread and wine; He was the priest of God Most High. And He blessed him and said: 'Blessed be Abram of God Most High, possessor of heaven and earth; and blessed be God Most High,* who has delivered your enemies into your hand.' And he gave Him a tithe of all" (Genesis 14:18-20.) This is known as a Theophany. In Greek it is *(theophaneia)* meaning a visible manifestation of a deity.

Revelation 10:2-6&8-11

> "And He had a little book open in His hand. And He set His right foot on the sea and His left foot on the land, and cried with a loud voice, as when a lion roars. And when He cried out, seven thunders uttered their voices. Now when the seven thunders uttered their voices, I was about to write; but I heard a voice from heaven saying to me, "Seal up the things which the seven thunders uttered, and do not write them." And the Angel whom I saw standing on the sea and on the land lifted up His hand to heaven and swore by Him who lives forever and ever, who created heaven and the things that are in it, the earth and the things that are in it, and the sea and the things that are in it, that there should be delay no longer,"

> "Then the voice which I heard from heaven spoke to me again and said, "Go, take the little book which is open in the hand of the Angel who stands on the sea and on the earth." And I went to the Angel and said to Him, "Give me the little book." And He said to me, "Take and eat it; and it will make your stomach bitter, but it will be as sweet as honey in your mouth." And I took the little book out of the Angel's hand and ate it, and it was as sweet as honey in my mouth. But when I had eaten it, my stomach became bitter. And He said to me, "You must prophesy again before many peoples, nations, tongues, and kings."

The little book could be the book Daniel was told to seal up until the time of the end *not* the end of time. That book also is a book of woe, mourning and doom for Israel. When the angel showed Daniel the end times, it was so horrible he was sick and lamented for days.

[SEE ALSO: DANIEL 8:26&27; 12:4, 8&9]

As John ate the little book he saw the deliverance of his people, the final victory of the Lamb and the setting up of the kingdom; it was truly sweet as honey in his mouth. But when he saw the suffering and destruction that was to come upon Israel before God delivered them, the reign of the antichrist and the pouring out of the bowls; it was bitter to his soul.

The *mighty Angel* set His right foot upon the sea and His left foot on the land showing dominion over all the earth, land and sea.

[SEE ALSO: DANIEL 7:13&14; PHILIPPIANS 2:9-11]

The mighty Angel (Jesus) swears by Himself that this present age is over and a new era shall begin.

[SEE ALSO: GENESIS 22:15&16; HEBREWS 6:13]

Only God can call for the end of an age or for time to be no longer.

In the last sentence of Revelation 10:3 it says: *"and when he had cried, seven thunders uttered their voices."*

Notice again the number seven. Whatever the seven thunders uttered was perfect and complete and is unknown except to God, the angels and John. John was told to not write down what he heard, and was commanded not to speak of it.

Revelation 10:7

> *"But in the days of the sounding of the seventh angel, when he is about to sound, the mystery of God would be finished, as He declared to His servants the prophets."*

The key word in this verse is days. The blowing of the seventh trumpet includes the pouring out of all seven bowl judgments over a period of days. The bowl judgments cross over each other not waiting until the previous one finishes before the next one begins.

The word mystery appears several times in Scripture. It is a truth that God has kept hidden from mankind until now and is only possible for believers to understand by studying the word of God. Man's wisdom never has comprehended, nor ever will be able to comprehend these truths apart from the word of God and the inspiration of the Holy Spirit.

> What is the *mystery of God?* *"This mystery is that through the gospel the Gentiles are heirs together with Israel, members together of one body, and sharers together in the promise in Christ Jesus." (Ephesians 3:6)*

[SEE ALSO: ROMANS 16:25&26; EPHESIANS 1:9-14; COLOSSIANS 1:25-27; 2:2&3; I TIMOTHY 3:16]

The mystery of God is that the Gentiles also have the right to become heirs to the kingdom. The unbelievers using their physical mind, ears and eyes cannot comprehend the spectacular things in store for those who believe in Jesus. When the mystery is revealed to unbelievers during the seventh trumpet it will be too late and will be a judgment for them. As spectacularly wonderful, marvelous and beautiful it will be for believers in Christ when revealed, that is how heartbreaking, sorrowful and horrible it will be for the unbelievers because they will see the reality of what they are going to miss.

CHAPTER 11

Revelation 11:1&2a

> *"Then I was given a reed like a measuring rod. And the angel stood, saying, "Rise and measure the temple of God, the altar, and those who worship there. But leave out the court which is outside the temple, and do not measure it, for it has been given to the Gentiles."*

John is no longer a bystander writing down what he sees but is again taking an active part in an event as he did in Revelation 10:9&10. He is handed a measuring rod 10½ feet long to measure the temple. The temple will be rebuilt by the Jews just before the seven year tribulation period begins and destroyed at the end of the seven year period.

The Old and New Testament show that the animal sacrifices will be offered for the first three and a half years in the temple. It will then be made desolate and be polluted by the antichrist, the very person with whom the Jews sign the seven year peace treaty.

> *"He will confirm a covenant with many for one 'seven' (seven years). In the middle of the 'seven' (three and a half years) he will put an end to sacrifice and offering. And on a wing of the temple he will set up an abomination that causes desolation, until the end that is decreed is poured out on him." (Daniel 9:27) (NIV)*

[SEE ALSO: DANIEL 12:7; 11&12; II THESSALONIANS 2:1-4]

Everything pertaining to the Jewish part of the temple and Old Testament type of worship will pass under the rod of judgment (even the people worshipping in the temple are measured with the rod) for the purpose of breaking the spirit of Israel and humbling them before Almighty God. The court of the Gentiles is not measured because it is defiled by the Gentiles (Muslims and other unbelievers). It is considered by God and the Jews to be polluted.

Revelation 11:2b

"And they will tread the holy city underfoot for forty-two months."

The temple the Jews build, though sanctioned by God, is a sign they still reject Jesus Christ as their Messiah. They return to sacrificing animals, still rejecting Christ's sacrifice at the cross and the shedding of His blood as the finished sacrifice for sin. The Jews are given permission to build the temple by the antichrist. When the seven year peace agreement is signed it marks the start of the *great tribulation*.

Ezekiel prophesied that the Jews will go back to Jerusalem in unbelief:

"I will show the holiness of My great name, which has been profaned among the nations, the name you have profaned among them. And the nations will know that I am the LORD, declares the Sovereign LORD, when I show Myself holy through you before their eyes for I will take you out of the nations; I will gather you from all the countries and bring you back into your own land." (Ezekiel 36:23&24)

The Jews build a temple in the name of Jehovah God, but they do not know Him and therefore must be cleansed through judgment.

Three and a half years into the great tribulation the antichrist will set himself up as god in the temple, this is the closest Satan will ever get to being like God.

In the first millennium B.C. Solomon built a spectacular temple in Jerusalem using the Lord's blueprints but it was ultimately destroyed by King Nebuchadnezzar of Babylon in 587B.C. It was rebuilt again by King Herod during Jesus time but destroyed again in 70A.D. by the Roman army led by General Titus. Titus did not leave one stone on top of another fulfilling Jesus prophesy:

> "The days will come upon you when your enemies will build an embankment against you and encircle you and hem you in on every side. They will dash you to the ground, you and the children within your walls. They will not leave one stone on another, because you did not recognize the time of God's coming to you." (Luke 19:43&44) (NIV)

[SEE ALSO: MATTHEW 24:2]

For many years scholars believed the temple would have to be rebuilt on the exact location where the present Mosque of Omar (Dome of the Rock) is standing. This would mean the mosque would have to be destroyed either through God's intervention, through some natural disaster or through war. It turns out this may not be the case at all.

Dr. Asher Kaufman a professor of physics at Hebrew University made some important archeological discoveries indicating the location of Solomon and Herod's temple was 26 meters (85 ft.31in.) away from the Dome of the Rock. If this is true the temple could be built without disturbing the mosque. Whether this is accurate or not, God's plan will be done and the temple will be rebuilt.

Revelation 11:3, 4&6

> *"And I will give power to My two witnesses, and they will prophesy one thousand two hundred and sixty days, clothed in sackcloth. These are the two olive trees and the two lampstands standing before the God of the earth."*
>
> *"These have power to shut heaven, so that no rain falls in the days of their prophesy; and they have power over waters to turn them to blood, and to strike the earth with all plagues, as often as they desire."*

The two olive trees and the two lampstands are symbolic of the two witnesses. There is controversy as to who the two witnesses might be since God does not reveal the names of both witnesses. He is clear that one of the witnesses is Elijah and gives direct clues as to who the second witness might be. Some people say they are *Moses* and *Elijah*, and some say *Elijah* and *Enoch*. These are the two most popular combinations. Other ideas are so out of context with scripture that they are not worth mentioning. What scripture reveals for certain is that they are wearing sackcloth as they witness like the prophets of the Old Testament did. They will be noticeably out of fashion for the 21st century, so people will regard them as weird. They will go throughout Jerusalem spreading the gospel to the Jews and remnant of the twelve tribes of Israel. Because of satellite, cable television, internet, computers, radio and whatever other technology may exist the entire world will be able to hear what these two witnesses say. They will preach God's word giving the world yet another chance to repent and come to Jesus.

In Old Testament times a prophet walking around in sackcloth was a sign of impending doom for Israel if they did not repent of their idolatrous ways and return to worshipping God. Prophets of

God were and are always 100% accurate. The Israelites usually killed their prophets because of their message.

[SEE ALSO: MATTHEW 23:37; LUKE 13:33&34]

The two witnesses are sent to Israel and though many will try, only the beast from the bottomless pit will be able to kill them. They are given their power by Jesus Himself for they are His witnesses. They will prophesy for 1,260 days (3½ years) by the Jewish calendar of 360 days to a year. The antichrist will be the supreme leader of the European Common Community and the Middle East at this time. In this same course of time Jerusalem will be trampled on by the antichrist's followers and many Jews will flee into the wilderness for protection.

Revelation 11:5a

> "And if anyone wants to harm them, fire proceeds from their mouth and devours their enemies."

Either these two witnesses will be able to breathe fire out of their mouths or they will be able to call fire down from heaven like Elijah did in *II Kings 1:9-12*.

Revelation 11:5b

> "And if anyone wants to harm them, he must be killed in this manner."

The people who will come against the two witnesses for the purpose of doing them harm will be killed by fire.

Revelation 11:7

> "Now when they finish their testimony, the beast that ascends out of the bottomless pit will make war against them, overcome them, and kill them."

The two witnesses will not be killed until they have finished their testimony. They can only be killed by the beast from the bottomless pit and only after a war takes place between them.

This is the first of 36 times the beast is mentioned in the *Book of Revelation*.

At this point, the person who is going to become the antichrist has been killed and the *"beast which ascended from the bottomless pit"* has taken possession of his body to make it look like he was raised from the dead. The antichrist is trying to deceive the world into thinking that he is God by imitating Jesus raised from the dead. A spectacular supernatural battle will take place between the two witnesses and the antichrist.

The world will love the person who will be the head of the European Common Community (ECC). He will be intelligent, have a magnetic personality, will be affluent and will seem to have the answers to solve all the problems of the world. He will unite the world with a false peace between Israel and the Arab nations at the beginning of the great tribulation. After he is killed it will look like he miraculously raised himself from the dead. He will now possess supernatural powers so that he will finally be able to kill the two witnesses who tormented the unbelievers for the last 42 months. The antichrist will be a hero in the eyes of the world.

Revelation 11:8-10

> *"And their dead bodies will lie in the street of the great city which spiritually is called Sodom and Egypt, where also our Lord was crucified. Then those from the peoples, tribes, tongues, and nations will see their dead bodies three and a half days, and not allow their dead bodies to be put into graves. And those who dwell on the earth will rejoice over*

> *them, make merry, and send gifts to one another, because these two prophets tormented those who dwell on the earth."*

The two witnesses are left lying dead in the street in the hot sun where the birds, animals and insects can feed on their carcasses in full view of the whole world. Their bodies will be defiled and mutilated for three and a half days. The entire earth rejoices. No one will be able to say when God raises them up that they weren't really dead. The antichrist is happy they are dead because of their prophesying, telling people what was still to come and warning them against the antichrist and of the return of Jesus. The beast had to shut them up.

Jerusalem will be so degenerated spiritually that scripture calls it *Sodom* and *Egypt*. Sodom is a symbol of immorality and Egypt is a symbol of materialism. The end of the verse *"where also our Lord was crucified"* leaves no doubt this is Jerusalem. The testimonies of these two witnesses are so strong they will be hated by the whole world. What would the world be like today if all believers were as powerful in witnessing and spreading the gospel?

Revelation 11:11

> *"Now after the three and a half days the breath of life from God entered them, and they stood on their feet, and great fear fell on those who saw them."*

Imagine the fear in everyone when after lying dead for three and a half days for the whole world to see, the Lord raises the two witnesses from the dead.

Revelation 11:12

> "And they heard a loud voice from heaven saying to them, "Come up here." And they ascended to heaven in a cloud and their enemies saw them."

After the breath of life enters into them they stand. God says to them *"come up here."* First they are resurrected then they are taken up to heaven in a cloud the same way Jesus ascended in Acts 1:9.

[SEE ALSO: DANIEL 7:13; I THESSALONIANS 4:17; REVELATION 1:7]

Revelation 11:13

> "In the same hour there was a great earthquake, and a tenth of the city fell. In the earthquake seven thousand men were killed, and the rest were afraid and gave glory to the God of heaven."

A tremendous earthquake takes place as soon as the two witnesses are taken into heaven. This quake is so powerful that it destroys one tenth of the city of Jerusalem and 7,000 people are killed. The rest of the people were scared to death by what they just saw and finally begin to glorify God. Unfortunately it is out of fear, not out of repentance. Though their hearts may be pounding in fear they are not breaking with conviction of their unrighteousness.

Revelation 11:14

> "The second woe is past. Behold, the third woe is coming quickly."

The sounding of the seventh trumpet includes everything that happens from this point up to *Revelation 23*.

Revelation 11:15

> "Then the seventh angel sounded: And there were loud voices in heaven, saying, "The kingdoms of this world have become the kingdoms of our Lord and of His Christ, and He shall reign forever and ever!""

The seventh angel blows his trumpet and the last terrifying three and a half years of the great tribulation begins. The seventh trumpet starts in heaven not with woes or terror but with rejoicing.

Jesus will rule during the millennium (1,000 years). After the millennium the Father will rule when Christ turns everything back over to Him. The sounding of the seventh trumpet marks the beginning of Christ's reign as King of kings and Lord of lord's. His priestly functions come to an end and His kingly duties begin. The angels finish the above verse with *"and He shall reign forever and ever."* His earthly reign begins when He returns to earth at the end of the great tribulation.

The seventh trumpet sounds over a period of time: *"in the days of the voice of the seventh angel, when he shall begin to sound"* (Revelation 10:7). The third woe includes all the bowls and judgments thru *Revelation 20*.

Revelation 11:16&17

> "And the twenty-four elders who sat before God on their thrones fell on their faces and worshipped God, saying: "We give You thanks, O Lord God Almighty, the One who is and who was and who is to come, because You have taken Your great power and reigned."

The twenty four elders worshipped Christ when the judgments began *(Revelation 5:8-10)* and they are worshipping Him now as the judgments are coming to an end. Those in heaven are rejoicing while those on earth are angry and full of hate.

Revelation 11:18a

> *"The nations were angry, and Your wrath has come,"*

All the nations are angry because God is pouring out His wrath upon the earth. His patience and long-suffering with unbelievers has come to an end.

Revelation 11:18b

> *"And the time of the dead, that they should be judged,"*

This refers to the white throne judgment at the end of the 1,000 year millennium. The unbelievers will be raised from the dead, judged and sentenced to their place in the Lake of Fire.

Revelation 11:18c

> *"And that You should reward Your servants the prophets and the saints,*
> *And those who fear Your name, small and great,"*

These will receive their reward of life everlasting with God.

Revelation 11:18d

> *"And should destroy those who destroy the earth."*

When the Lord comes back He will destroy those who followed the antichrist and destroyed the earth.

Revelation 11:19

> *"Then the temple of God was opened in heaven, and the ark of His covenant was seen in His temple. And there were lightnings, noises, thunderings, an earthquake, and great hail."*

Chapter 11

What a spectacular sight this must have been for John to see the "Ark Of The Covenant" in God's temple.

When the temple is opened there is lightning, noises and thunder which represent judgment. A great earthquake shakes the earth along with great hail. When Jesus died on the cross there was a great earthquake and a violent storm with thunder and lightning. The temple was opened when the veil tore in half from top to bottom. *(Matthew 27:50&51)*

CHAPTER 12

Revelation 12:1&2

> *"Now a great sign appeared in heaven: a woman clothed with the sun, with the moon under her feet, and on her head a garland of twelve stars. Then being with child, she cried out in labor and in pain to give birth."*

The woman is a symbolic representation of the nation of Israel (Genesis 3:15). Israel is compared to a woman in scripture (Isaiah 54:1-8). The promised seed (Jesus) was to come through Israel. Israel's travails and pains do not come till *after* Christ is born.

> *"Before she travailed, she brought forth; before her pain came, she was delivered of a man child."* (Isaiah 66:7)(KJV)

Revelation 12:3

> *"And another sign appeared in heaven: behold, a great, fiery red dragon having seven heads and ten horns, and seven diadems on his heads."*

The creature symbolizes Satan. His color as a dragon is fiery red affiliating him with blood and death. The seven heads represent the seven world kingdoms that have ruled the earth (Egypt, Assyria, Babylon, Medo–Persia, Greece, Rome and the revived Roman Empire (E.C.C.). The seven diadems (crowns) show Satan controlled these kingdoms.

The seventh head represents the Roman Empire in the end times and the 10 horns represent the 10 nations of the revived Roman Empire (E.C.C.).

God told Satan in the Garden of Eden: *"And I will put enmity (war) between you (Satan) and the woman (Mary), and between your offspring (antichrist) and hers (Christ); He (Jesus) will crush your (Satan) head, and you will strike His heal."* (Genesis 3:15) From that day forward Satan tried every means possible to destroy the lineage of the promised seed. If Satan succeeded he could say that the scriptures were false, showing God to be a liar. Satan could then claim mankind for himself since there would be no means of salvation through Christ.

The beast with seven heads, ten horns and seven crowns is associated with the "beast out of the sea" of Revelation 13:1 but is not the same beast. The dragon's crowns are on his *heads*, while the beast out of the sea crowns is on his *horns*. The crowns on the heads of the dragon reveal Satan has reigned over the seven world kingdoms until Christ returns to sit on the throne of David.

Revelation 12:4a

> *"His tail drew a third of the stars of heaven and threw them to the earth."*

This verse refers to Genesis where Satan showed his cunning and deceitful heart by convincing one third of the heavenly host (represented here as stars) to rebel against God and follow him. Satan's army of angels was cast to the earth until their final judgment when they will be cast into the Lake of Fire forever.

Revelation 12:4b

> "And the dragon stands before the woman who was ready to give birth, to devour her Child as soon as it was born."

Satan is the eternal enemy of Israel. The verb is *stands* not stood. It refers to a continuous act and not to a mere passing event. The moment the word went forth that the seed of the woman should one day crush the serpent's head; Satan took his stand before the woman in order to destroy her seed as soon as He should be born.

Revelation 12:5

> "And she bore a male Child who was to rule all nations with a rod of iron. And her Child was caught up to God and to His throne."

Jesus lineage was of the house of David, the lion of the tribe of Judah. He is to rule all nations and He will destroy the evil nations with the iron scepter.

> "You will rule them with an iron scepter; you will dash them to pieces like a pottery." (Psalms 2:9) (NIV)

For Israel He will use the iron scepter to mold and shape them for His will.

> "Yet, O LORD, You are our Father. We are the clay, and You are the potter; we are all the work of Your hand." (Isaiah 64:8) (NIV)

[SEE ALSO: JEREMIAH 18:6; REVELATION 2:27; 19:15]

These verses reveal Christ's rule will be autocratic not tyrannical. Christ will be Supreme. His rule will be a rule of love that is fair, just and honest. Politics will not be found in the government. The people will not be oppressed by those in power and equal rights will be given to everyone.

God is dealing strictly with Israel in this part of the book. Not even a hint of the church is found here. This parallels the *seventy weeks of Daniel*, which predicts four hundred and eighty three (483) years, or (69 weeks of years) until *"Messiah the Prince shall be cut off (crucified)"*. Then, making no reference to the two thousand (2,000) year Church Age continues on to the Jewish seven year great tribulation period, completing the *seventy weeks of years*.
[SEE ALSO: DANIEL 9:23-27]

Between verses five and six of Revelation 12; 2,000 years of Christianity (church history) takes place. Verse five encompasses Christ's birth to His death; while verse six takes place during the tribulation period which is still future.

The woman, which represents Israel, flees into the wilderness where God has prepared a place for her. Just as God provided for Israel forty years in the wilderness during Moses time, He will provide for Israel during the tribulation for 1,260 days. Scripture speaks of a world war taking place in the middle of the tribulation period to once again try to eliminate the nation of Israel and the Jewish race forever.
[SEE ALSO: DANIEL 11:40-44]

Three Middle East countries escape harm: Edom, Moab and Ammon which is present day Jordan *(Daniel 11:41)*. This could be the wilderness where Israel will flee to for protection during the last three and a half years of the great tribulation.

The overall picture presented in *Revelation 12* illustrates Satan being cast down waiting for the woman (Israel) to deliver and the beast trying to destroy Israel with all the power of the nations under his control. No earthly nation will have the power to protect Israel or be able to blind the world to where Israel will be hidden. It can only be through supernatural powers from our LORD. If the

LORD could protect Israel for forty years in the desert in Old Testament times, He can surely protect them for three and a half years in the end times.

Revelation 12:7-9

> *"And war broke out in heaven: Michael and his angels fought against the dragon; and the dragon and his angels fought, but they did not prevail, nor was a place found for them in heaven any longer. So the great dragon was cast out, that serpent of old, called the Devil and Satan, who deceives the whole world; he was cast to the earth, and his angels were cast out with him."*

Satan and his angels will be cast out from heavenly places and be grounded to the earth until the time of there judgment. There are two main names to identify Satan although there are others. In the Old Testament he is mostly known as Satan while in the New Testament he generally is called Devil. Satan in Hebrew means *"to attack"*, to be *"an adversary"*. In the Greek language it means *"the accuser"*. Devil in the Greek is *"diabolos"* and means *"false accuser"* and *"slanderer"*. Even now Satan accuses us before God (Revelation 12:10b). Satan may be the *ruler of this world*, but Satan is not the God of this earth. The earth belongs to its maker, Jesus Christ, who spoke it into existence. Satan is the god of the world systems that embrace business, society, politics, religion, money and any other material things. He is the ruler of the powers of darkness of the spirit world.

> *"For we wrestle not against flesh and blood, but against principalities, against powers, against the rulers of the darkness of this world, against spiritual wickedness in high places."(Ephesians 6:12)*

Satan is so powerful, Michael the archangel commander of God's heavenly host dared not challenge him in a conflict by his own abilities but knew he needed to use the Lord's name to fight him *(Jude 9)*. This should be a lesson to us all. If Michael the archangel needed God's strength to battle Satan then we must also go to God in prayer and supplication. Our strength comes from Jesus Christ and not from ourselves.

Scripture says Satan is a king and has a kingdom.
[SEE ALSO: EZEKIEL 28:12,13A&14; MATTHEW 12:25&26; MARK 3:23-26]

Satan knows once he is cast down to the earth that he only has three and a half years until he is chained in the bottomless pit for one thousand years. He will go on a rampage to make hell on earth for the inhabitants who are left. God's wrath will also be pouring out on the earth at the same time.

Revelation 12:10a

> *"Then I heard a loud voice saying in heaven, "Now salvation, and strength, and the kingdom of our God, and the power of His Christ have come,"*

This is the same loud voice heard in *Revelation 6:9-11*. They compliment and parallel each other. The *"little season"* God told the souls under the sea of glass to wait is now over. The request from these souls is now answered.

Revelation 6 said that the souls under the altar were: *"slain for the word of God and their testimony which they held"*. In Revelation 12:11 the loud voices were the ones who overcame Satan by the: *"blood of the Lamb and by the word of their testimony"*, exactly as in *Revelation 6:9-11*.

Revelation 12:10b

> *"For the accuser of our brethren, who accused them before our God day and night, has been cast down."*

Satan has been making accusations since Old Testament day's right up to the present time (Job 1:9-11). He accused Job before God. He could only see the material wealth of Job but God saw Job's spiritual wealth. Job knew material things were just extras from God. All we have belongs to the LORD. We are caretakers of the things God gives us.

> *"Naked I came from my mother's womb, and naked, I will depart. The Lord gave, and the Lord has taken away; may the name of the Lord be praised."* (Job 1:21) (NIV)

The accuser of our brethren is cast down and he is going to strike with a vengeance especially against Israel.

Revelation 12:11

> *"And they overcame him by the blood of the Lamb and by the word of their testimony, and they did not love their lives to the death."*

This verse reveals the three fold way in which we can defeat Satan in our everyday lives.

1. Overcome him *"by the blood of the Lamb."* The tribulation martyrs will realize what believers knew all along; that there is power in the blood of Jesus. It is the "blood" that washes us clean; Jesus died so we could live.

[SEE ALSO: ISAIAH 1:18]

2. *"By the word of their testimony"* Nothing infuriates Satan more than a believer willing to stand up and boldly proclaim

his love for Jesus Christ and share his victory over sin because of Christ's sacrifice on the cross.

[SEE ALSO: LUKE 12:8&9; JOHN 10:10]

3. "They loved not their lives unto death". How strong are you? If your life was in jeopardy by saying "Yes, I am a Christian" would you be strong and courageous enough to say it?

[SEE ALSO: REVELATION 20:4B]

What will be the reward for this total rejection of Satan? *"And they lived and reigned with Christ a thousand years."* (Revelation 20:4c)

What must have been going through John's head as he watched 21st century martyrs tortured and killed much the same way they were in his day? This must have been terrifying for him to realize that 2,000 years into the future the persecution of Christian and Jews would still be going on. At the same time, how uplifting it must have been for John to see Christianity still going strong after 2,000 years. Believers were still willing to die for their faith in the 21st century for an unseen God.

Revelation 12:12a

"Therefore rejoice, O heavens, and you who dwell in them."

What a glorious time for the saints, martyrs and God's holy angels. All the heavens and everything in them will rejoice. The Devil can no longer stand before the throne of God accusing believers. No longer will Satan be able to fly through the heavens polluting and corrupting wherever he goes.

"Then he showed me Joshua the high priest standing before the Angel of the LORD, and Satan standing at his right hand to oppose him. And the LORD said to Satan, 'The LORD rebukes you, Satan! The LORD who has chosen Je-

rusalem rebukes you! Is this not a brand plucked from the fire?'"(Zechariah 3:1&2)

[SEE ALSO: EPHESIANS 2:1-3]

For the angels of God there will finally be peace. The war they have been fighting with Satan for thousands of years is over. It is not a truce, or a peace agreement, it is a total victory over Satan. Michael the archangel and his army have won. There is peace in heaven forever and Satan with his army is confined to the earth until the judgment day.

[SEE ALSO: ISAIAH 14:12-17; LUKE 11:17&18A]

Revelation 12:12b

"Woe to the inhabitants of the earth and of the sea! For the devil has come down to you, having great wrath, because he knows that he has a short time."

While heaven is rejoicing, the earth is crying. The devil with his army of angels and demons are confined permanently to the earth. *"He has great wrath"* Satan knows he has only three and a half years left before he is chained and imprisoned for 1,000 years.

This is one of the reasons Satan wants to keep people from reading the Book of Revelation more than any other book of the Bible. It reveals Satan loses and any one who chose to follow him also loses in the end. Satan now goes on a rampage and releases all his anger and fury against Israel. He will try to accomplish what ancient Rome and Hitler failed to do which is to annihilate the Jews from the face of the earth.

Revelation 12:13

"Now when the dragon saw that he had been cast to the earth, he persecuted the woman who gave birth to the male Child."

The antichrist tries to destroy Israel but his ultimate failure was prophesied in *Isaiah 10:24-26; 14:6&7, 9-12&15; Jeremiah 30:7-9; Daniel 8:23-25; 11:36.*

Revelation 12:14

> "But the woman was given two wings of a great eagle, that she might fly into the wilderness to her place, where she is nourished for a time and times and half a time, from the presence of the serpent."

One third of the Israelites will flee into the wilderness with the supernatural help of God. They will be protected for three and a half years. Only by divine intervention could the Israelites be hidden from Satan for that length of time. The remaining believers and Israelites who convert to Christianity during this time will stand against the antichrist rather than flee.

Some people believe that because this verse says she was given *"two wings of a great eagle"*, the United States (because our symbol is the Bald Eagle) is going to airlift Israel into the secret place in the wilderness but scriptures reveal this is not true.

> "You have seen what I did to the Egyptians, and how I bore you (Israel) on eagles' wings and brought you to Myself."(Exodus 19:4)

> "As an eagle stirs up its nest, hovers over its young, spreading out its wings, taking them up carrying them on its wings, so the LORD alone led him (Israel), and there was no foreign god with him." (Deuteronomy 32:11&12)

No one, not the United States nor any other nation will be able to take the credit for this exodus into the wilderness. The world will know this is divine intervention and Israel is under the protection of the hand of God. After all the disasters have happened that are written in this book, it is unlikely that the United States or any other nation will have the resources to feed themselves let alone another nation.

> Isaiah 26:20 speaks of this time when Israel will flee into their place: "Come, My people, enter your chambers, and shut your doors behind you; hide yourself, as it were, for a little moment, until the indignation is past."

Revelation 12:15

> "So the serpent spewed water out of his mouth like a flood after the woman that he might cause her to be carried away by the flood."

This flood is symbolic of a massive army the antichrist will send after Israel.

> "This is what the LORD says: "See how the waters are rising in the north; they will become an overflowing torrent. They will overflow the land and everything in it, the towns and those who live in them. The people will cry out; all who dwell in the land will wail at the sound of the hoofs of galloping steeds, at the noise of enemy chariots and the rumble of their wheels. Fathers will not turn to help their children; their hands will hang limp." (Jeremiah 47:2&3)(NIV)

[SEE ALSO: ISAIAH 59:19; JEREMIAH 46:7&8; DANIEL 11:22&26]

In whose territory will Israel be allowed to hide in? Reference is made to Moab as being Israel's protector at this time. Moab is commanded to welcome Israel (the outcasts) and not betray her to the antichrist. This area is the wilderness where Israel wandered in the desert for forty years with Moses.

[SEE ALSO: DEUTERONOMY 2:9&19; ISAIAH 16:3&4]

Revelation 12:16

> "But the earth helped the woman, and the earth opened its mouth and swallowed up the flood which the dragon had spewed out of his mouth"

Once again divine intervention saves Israel and destroys Satan's army. God will open the earth and swallow the army like He did in Numbers 16: 30-33.

Revelation 12:17

> "And the dragon was enraged with the woman, and he went to make war with the rest of her offspring, who keep the commandments of God and have the testimony of Jesus Christ."

Satan is furious. The armies he sent after the fleeing Israelites are destroyed. What does Satan do next? If he can't have all the Israelites, he'll take his vengeance out on those who did not flee. The verse says the dragon makes war with those who "*keep the commandments of God (Jews), and have the testimony of Jesus Christ (believers).*"

Satan will try to slaughter all remaining believers in Jesus Christ. The last of the martyrs are about to be killed and the cries which went up from the saints in Revelation 6:11 are now going to be answered.

CHAPTER 13

Revelation 13:1

> "Then I stood on the sand of the sea. And I saw a beast rising up out of the sea, having seven heads and ten horns, and on his horns ten crowns, and on his heads a blasphemous name."

The beast is symbolic. It is the same beast Daniel saw in his vision.

> "After this I saw in the night visions, and behold, a fourth beast, dreadful and terrible, exceedingly strong. It had huge iron teeth; it was devouring, breaking in pieces, and trampling the residue with its feet. It was different from all the beasts that were before it, and it had ten horns." (Daniel 7:7)

The sea is symbolic of people and nations.

> "And he said to me, "The waters which you saw, where the harlot sits, are peoples, multitudes, nations, and tongues." (Revelation 17:15)

When John says he *"stood on the sand of the sea"*, he is referring to the Mediterranean Sea. The beast has a two fold meaning: it is rising up from the Mediterranean Sea, but John also sees it as a person (antichrist) rising up from among many nations. The absolute identification of who the antichrist is will not be known until he signs the seven year peace covenant between Israel and the Arab nations.

> "And he shall confirm the covenant with many for one week (seven years)." (Daniel 9:27a)

He is called the antichrist because he is opposed to, or the opposite of everything that Christ represents. This evil monster is known by many titles in the bible.

Old Testament

1. The Assyrian: *Isaiah 10:5&6; 30:31*
2. King of Babylon: *Isaiah 14:4*
3. Lucifer: *Isaiah 14:12*
4. King of Tyrus: *Ezekiel 28:12-15*
5. The Little Horn: *Daniel 7:8; 8:9-12*
6. King of Fierce Countenance: *Daniel 8:23*
7. Prince That Shall Come: *Daniel 9:26*
8. The Willful King: *Daniel 11:36*

New Testament

1. Man of Sin; Son of Perdition; That Wicked One: *IIThessalonians 2:3-9*
2. Antichrist: *1 John 2:18*
3. The Beast: *Revelation 13:1a&2; John 5:43*

There are fourteen "contrasts" between Jesus Christ and the antichrist in the Scriptures.

1. Christ came from above: *John 6:38*
   Antichrist will ascend from the pit: *Revelation 11:7*
2. Christ came in His Fathers name: *John 5:43*
   Antichrist will come in his own name: *John 5:43*
3. Christ humbled Himself: *Philippians 2:8*
   Antichrist will exalt himself: *II Thessalonians 2:4*
4. Christ was despised: *Isaiah 53:3; Luke 23:18*
   Antichrist will be admired: *Revelation 13:3&4*

5. Christ will be exalted: *Philippians 2:9*
    Antichrist will be cast down to hell: Isaiah 14:14&15

6. Christ came to do His Father's will: *John 6:38*
    Antichrist will come to do his own will: Daniel 11:36

7. Christ came to save: *Luke 19:10*
    Antichrist will come to destroy: Daniel 8:24

8. Christ is the Good Shepherd: *John 10:1-15*
    Antichrist is the idol (evil shepherd): Zechariah 11:16&17

9. Christ is the True Vine: *John 15:1*
    Antichrist is the vine of the earth: Revelation 14:18

10. Christ is "The Truth": *John 14:6*
    Antichrist is "The Lie": II Thessalonians 2:11

11. Christ is the "Holy One": *Mark 1:24*
    Antichrist is the "Man of Sin": II Thessalonians 2:3

12. Christ is "The Man of Sorrows": *Isaiah 53:3*
    Antichrist is the "Man of Sin": II Thessalonians 2:3

13. Christ is the "Son of God": *Luke 1:35*
    Antichrist is the "Son of Perdition": II Thessalonians 2:3

14. Christ is the "Mystery of Godliness": God manifest in the-Flesh: *I Timothy 3:16*
    Antichrist is the "Mystery of Iniquity": Satan manifest in the Flesh – II Thessalonians 2:3&7

The antichrists nationality will be a mixture. He *rises up out of the Mediterranean Sea* meaning he comes from an area of many nationalities, so he will be part Gentile.

Daniel 8:8&9 reveals he is the little horn which comes out of one of the four horns (Greece was divided among Alexander the Greats four generals after his death); and it will be revealed in the scriptures the antichrist is from Syria.

"Therefore the he goat waxed very great (Alexander the Great conquered the world): and when he was strong, the great horn was broken (Alexander the Great drank himself to death); and for it came up four notable ones (Alexander's four generals) toward the four winds of heaven (they split his kingdom in quarters between themselves). And out of one of them (Syria) came forth a little horn (the antichrist), which waxed exceeding great, toward the south, and toward the east, and toward the pleasant land (Jerusalem)."

Antichrist's Bloodline

Daniel 9:26b "*and the people of the prince that shall come (Roman Empire; present day European Common Community) shall destroy the city (Jerusalem) and the sanctuary (Jewish Temple)."* He will be the leader of the E.C.C.

Daniel 11:37a "*Neither shall he regard the God of his fathers"* reveals that he will also be part Jewish. Israel will trust signing a peace treaty with someone who has Jewish blood in him. The antichrist will be a Syrian Jew of Grecian descent.

The beast that John sees has seven heads, which also has a dual meaning:

1. The beast will rule the revived Roman Empire; Rome sits on seven hills.
2. The seven heads represent the seven kings who ruled the Roman Empire. There were five kings who ruled up to the time of John. The sixth king, Domitian, was the Roman king who put John into exile on the Isle of Patmos, and the seventh king will be the antichrist ruling the E.C.C. before he is slain.

"And I saw one of his heads as it was wounded (slain) to death"; it is the seventh king who is slain. (Revelation 13:3)

All the beast's heads are fine when he comes up out of the sea. It is after the beast is out of the sea that John sees "one head is

wounded unto death; but the deadly wound is healed."
(Revelation 13:1)

Revelation 17:11 He is called *"the beast that was, and is not, is himself also the eighth, and is of the seven, and is going to perdition."* The seventh king (the human antichrist) is killed at the end of the first three and a half years of the tribulation. The beast out of the bottomless pit will possess the body of the seventh king who was slain and become the eighth king. By this Satan tries to imitate the resurrection of Christ and thus makes the world to *"wonder after the beast"*. (Revelation 13:3)

The ten horns on the beast in Daniel 7:7&8 and on John's beast in Revelation 13:1-7 represent the "ten toes" made of iron and clay in King Nebuchadnezzar's image in Daniel 2:33&42 *"His legs of iron, his feet part of iron and part of clay."*

> *"And as the toes of the feet were part of iron, and part of clay, so the kingdom shall be partly strong, and partly broken."*

They are the ten kingdoms that made up the Old Roman Empire, which are in existence today known as the "European Common Community (ECC)". Because all these nations are united under the E.C.C. they have strength with one common currency the Euro-dollar. Yet it is unstable because not all the people like being united under one common name. They fear losing their individual identity, culture and ethnicity. (Ex: British, French, and German etc.)

When the beast from the bottomless pit is first released he has seven heads and ten horns but they are not crowned because he has not yet possessed the dead body of the (human) antichrist (Revelation 17:12).

The beast which comes out of the sea in Revelation 13:1 has its ten horns crowned. This reveals the beast at the height of his power when he gives the heads of the ten nations the power to be kings but it will be short lived.

> "And the ten horns which you saw are ten kings who have received no kingdom as yet, but they receive authority for one hour as kings with the beast. These are of one mind, and they will give their power and authority (They will turn over all their armies to the command of the antichrist) to the beast." (Revelation 17:12&13)

Revelation 13:2

> "Now the beast which I saw was like a leopard, his feet were like the feet of a bear, and his mouth like the mouth of a lion. And the dragon gave him his power, his throne, and great authority."

Explanation of images from Nebuchadnezzar's dream, Daniel and John's vision

John describes the creature he sees as a beast, leopard, bear, and lion; which is the opposite of Daniels vision of lion, bear, leopard and beast and of King Nebuchadnezzar's dream of head of gold, chest & arms of silver, waist & hips of bronze, and legs of iron.

I will take Daniels vision and explain each animal scripturally one by one starting with the lion.

> "You, O king, were watching; and behold, a great image! This great image, whose splendor was excellent, stood before you; and its form was awesome.
>
> This image's head was of fine gold, its chest and arms of silver, its belly and thighs of bronze, its legs of iron, its feet partly of iron and partly of clay." (Daniel 2:31-33 & 36-38)
>
> "This is the dream. Now we will tell the interpretation of it before the king.

Chapter 13

You, O king, are a king of kings. For the God of heaven has given you a kingdom, power, strength, and glory;
And wherever the children of men dwell, or the beasts of the field and the birds of the heaven, He has given them into your hand, and has made you ruler over them all-you are this head of gold."

The Babylonian empire lasted from 605B.C. to 538B.C. (69 years) and the city of Babylon covered more than 2,000 acres located along the Euphrates River (present day Iraq).

King Nebuchadnezzar was an absolute monarch.

The governing powers of this image deteriorate just as the value of the image and the weight of the image deteriorates from the head to the toes. The value of gold is more precious than silver, silver more than brass, brass more than iron; and their specific weight declines as well, making the image top heavy. The density in grams of gold = 19.5, silver = 10.47, brass = 8, iron = 5, and clay = 1.93.

It is by understanding this image that we can understand the meaning of the wild beasts of Daniel and John's visions.

"The first was like a lion, and had eagle's wings. I watched till its wings were plucked off; and it was lifted up from the earth and made to stand on two feet like a man, and a man's heart was given to it." (Daniel 7:4)

The combination of the lion (king of beasts) and the eagle (king of birds) correspond to the swiftness of Nebuchadnezzar's armies. Babylon's coat of arms was then and is now a "lion with eagle's wings standing on its feet having the head of a man". They can be seen today in the British museum in London, on the archeological stones dug up from the front gates of Nebuchadnezzar's castle and the hanging gardens of Babylon that were being rebuilt by Sodom Hussein, the leader of Iraq, until his capture by American forces in 2004.

The plucking of the wings refers to the beastly insanity God caused to come upon King Nebuchadnezzar for seven years until he acknowledged God as the only true God.
[DANIEL 4:16, 24-26, 33; 5:18-21]

The lifting up and causing to stand on its feet like a man, refers to king Nebuchadnezzar's restoration back to sanity once he acknowledged God as the only true God.
[DANIEL 4:34-37]

The second beast of Daniel's vision was like a bear:

> *"And suddenly another beast, a second, like a bear. It was raised up on one side, and had three ribs in its mouth between its teeth. And they said thus to it: 'Arise, devour much flesh!' (Daniel 7:5)*

This beast coincides with Nebuchadnezzar's image of: "chest and arms of silver."

The bear is the strongest beast after the lion and is noted for its voracity, but has none of the agility and majesty of the lion. A bear is awkward in its movements and accomplishes its purpose by brute force and sheer strength.

These were the characteristics of the Medo-Persian army. It did not gain its victories by bravery or skill, but overwhelmed its enemies with vast numbers of troops. Xerxes expedition against Greece was undertaken with 2,500,000 fighting men, and when including the camp followers, made an army of 5,000,000. You can read why, when and how the bear (Medo-Persia) devoured the lion (Babylon) in Daniel 5:1-31.

The raised side of the bear signifies Persia which held the greater military strength and corresponded to the right shoulder and arm of Nebuchadnezzar's giant. The three ribs stand for the three kingdoms of Babylon, Lydia, and Egypt which formed a triple alliance that tried to defeat the Medo-Persian army but were destroyed.

Persia was an empire which at its height stretched from Greece in the west to India in the east. The Persian Empire came into power with the victory of Cyrus the Great over his Medan overlord Darius in 550B.C. and lasted until the conquest of Alexander the Great in 330B.C.

The third beast of Daniels vision was like a leopard:

> "After this I looked, and there was another, like a leopard, which had on its back four wings of a bird. The beast also had four heads, and dominion was given to it." (Daniel 7:6)

The leopard is a swift and graceful creature and its speed here is further assisted by wings. The frame of a leopard is slight but strong, swift and fierce. These characteristics made it a fitting symbol of the Greeks under the leadership of Alexander the Great, who, followed by a small but very well-equipped and extremely brave army moved with great speed and overthrew the forces of Persia and conquered the entire civilized world.

The four wings of a bird symbolize a fowl. Just as a fowl can't fly very high, the armies of Alexander were fitted mainly for low land fighting. They also symbolize the four quarters of the earth to which Alexander extended his kingdom.

The four heads of the leopard represent the four kingdoms which Alexander's Empire was divided into by his four generals. Alexander drank himself to death at the age of 32 out of boredom after he conquered the world.

The leopard corresponds to the belly and thighs of bronze in Nebuchadnezzar's Giant.

> "his belly and his thighs of brass."
> "And another third kingdom of brass, which shall bear rule over all the earth." (Daniel 2:32c&39b)

The leopard is the dominant beast in John's vision revealing that the antichrist will be of Grecian descent from Syria *(Daniel 11)* and will rule the Old Roman Empire, known today as the E.C.C. (European Common Community).

The fourth beast was unlike any beast that Daniel had ever seen or heard about and the same holds true for the beast that John sees. The fourth beast in Daniel 7:7 and Revelation 13:2 coincides with Nebuchadnezzar's image:

> "Its legs of iron, its feet partly of iron and partly of clay"
> "And the fourth kingdom shall be as strong as iron, inasmuch as iron breaks in pieces and shatters all things; and like iron that crushes, that kingdom will break in pieces and crush all the others." (Daniel 2:33&40)

The fourth beast has iron teeth with ten horns on its head. The iron teeth correspond to the iron legs, and the ten horns to the ten toes of Nebuchadnezzar's image and symbolize the fourth world empire-- Rome.

> "I was considering the horns, and there was another horn, a little one, coming up among them, before whom three of the first horns were plucked out by the roots. And there, in this horn, were eyes like the eyes of a man, and a mouth speaking pompous words." (Daniel 7:8)

> "I, Daniel, was grieved in my spirit within my body, and the visions of my head troubled me." (Daniel 7:15)

Daniel saw nothing corresponding to the little horn on Nebuchadnezzar's image. He realized this was some new revelation that

God did not want the Gentile king Nebuchadnezzar to see, but was reserved for Daniel and the Jews.

The last six (6) chapters of the book of Daniel deal strictly with the Jews of the end times.

> "Now I have come to make you understand what will happen to your people (Jews) in the latter days, for the vision refers to many days yet to come." (Daniel 10:14)

Daniel was greatly troubled by this vision of the horn and was curious as to its meaning. He asked one of the angels that stood by him to tell him the meaning. Daniel was told plainly that the four beasts represent four kings (kingdoms). Daniel persisted and wanted to know the truth about the fourth beast that was so different from the other three and so unlike anything he had ever seen before and he especially wanted to know about the little horn. He was told that the ten horns on the fourth beast represented ten kingdoms that shall arise and that the little horn was a king who should rise from among them and subdue three of them who would not want to submit to his power. Daniel was told this king would be a person of remarkable intelligence and have great oratorical skills with a mouth speaking great things. This person would be audacious, arrogant, persecuting and seek to change "times and laws" and that the "saints of the Most High" (Daniels people [Jews]) would be given into his hands for "a time, and times, and the dividing of time (3½ years)" (Daniel 7:25).

In this vision of the four beasts can be seen a degeneration just as it was in the metals of Nebuchadnezzar's image. The descent goes from the "lion" a majestic king of beasts to a terrible "monster" that defies description.

King Nebuchadnezzar saw these four kingdoms represented as a magnificent image made of precious metals but Daniels vision and John's vision shows them as a succession of wild beasts. It shows the difference between mans view of the world and God's view of the world. Man sees wealth, majesty and power but God sees it as a succession of wild beasts devouring one another.

It is Satan who gives the antichrist (the beast) his power and authority and throne but it is God who allows Satan to do it. The beast will be living on borrowed time loaned to him by God. Notice in Revelation 13:5&7 how the beast received his power.

The beast "was given" a mouth speaking great things and blasphemies.

Power "was given" unto him to continue forty and two months (if it was Satan in control, he certainly wouldn't limit himself to only forty two months).

He "was given" power to make war with the saints, and to overcome them.

Power "was given" him over every tribe, tongue, and nation.

God is allowing the antichrist to have power for this short span of time for the purpose of fulfilling the scriptures and God's ultimate plan for mankind. He has Satan on a leash, just like in the Book of Job; Satan can only do what God allows him to.

Nebuchadnezzar's Dream (Babylon)	Daniel's Vision (Babylon)	John's Vision (Babylon)
Head of gold	Lion with eagle wings. Wings were plucked. Made to stand as a man. Given a mans heart.	Mouth of a lion
(Medo-Persia)	**(Medo-Persia)**	**(Medo-Persia)**
Breast & arms of silver	Bear raised up on one side. Three ribs in his mouth. Three ribs in his mouth	Feet of a bear
(Greece)	**(Greece)**	**(Greece)**
Belly & thighs of brass	Leopard with four wings & four heads	Main body of a leopard
(Rome)	**(Rome)**	**(Rome)**
Legs of iron; feet & toes partly Iron & partly clay	Dreadful & terrible beast. Great iron teeth	Beast with 7 heads & ten horns

Greece: Alexander's four generals (four heads) split his kingdom after his death:

1. Cassander – Greece & Macedoni
2. Lysimachus – Turkey & Thrace (Asia Minor)
3. Seleucus – Syria & Babylon (Iraq)
4. Ptolemy – Egypt

These four divisions are present day Greece, Turkey, Syria and Egypt.

> "I saw one of his heads as if it had been mortally wounded, and his deadly wound was healed. And all the world marveled and followed the beast." (Revelation 13:3)

The antichrist will be killed by an assassin then the beast from the bottomless pit will possess the antichrist's body. Many become followers of the beast because of this amazing restoration. This will be at the end of the first three and a half years of the seven year great tribulation.

Revelation 13:4
> "So they worshipped the dragon who gave authority to the beast; and they worshiped the beast, saying, 'Who is like the beast? Who is able to make war with him?'"

The world will accept the antichrist and worship Satan as God. When God manifested Himself to us through His Son, Jesus Christ the world rejected Him, even though Christ performed countless miracles.

> "And there are also many other things which Jesus did, the which, if they should be written every one, I suppose that even the world itself could not contain the books that should be written. Amen" (John 21:25).

> Jesus prophesied: "I have come in My Father's name, and you do not receive Me; if another comes in his own name, him you will receive" (John 5:43).

Jesus has many titles in the Scriptures.

Isaiah 9:6b "And His name shall be called, Wonderful, Counselor, Mighty God, Everlasting Father, Prince of Peace."

I Corinthians 15:45 "Last Adam"

Revelation 21:6 "Alpha & Omega"

John 6:35 "Bread of Life"

Ephesians 2:20 "Chief Cornerstone"

I Peter 5:4 "Chief Shepherd"

Colossians 1:18 "First Born from the Dead"

John 10:11 "Good Shepherd"

Hebrews 13:20 "Great Shepherd of the sheep"

Hebrews 3:1 "High Priest"

Mark 1:24 "Holy One of God"

Matthew 1:23 "Immanuel"

Revelation 19:16 "King of kings"

Revelation 19:16 "Lord of lords"

John 1:29 "Lamb of God"

John 9:5 "Light of the World"

I Corinthians 2:8 "Lord of Glory"

I Timothy 2:5 "Mediator between God and men"

John 1:14 "Only Begotten of the Father"

Acts 3:22 "Prophet"

Luke 1:47 "Savior"

Galatians 3:16 "Seed of Abraham"

Matthew 18:11 "Son of man"

John 1:1 "The Word"

The people worship the antichrist believing he is God. Who can defeat him? He was murdered and was raised from the dead.

Revelation 13:5&6

> "And he was given a mouth speaking great things and blasphemies, and he was given authority to continue for for-

> ty-two months. Then he opened his mouth in blasphemy against God, to blaspheme His name, His tabernacle, and those who dwell in heaven."

Satan gives the antichrist the ability to speak eloquently to deceive the people and at the same time curse God. The persecution of the new believers and the Jews will be unlike anything seen before in the history of mankind.

[SEE ALSO: REVELATION 20:4B]

Revelation 13:7&8

> "And it was granted to him to make war with the saints and to overcome them. And authority was given him over every tribe, tongue, and nation. And all who dwell on the earth will worship him, whose names have not been written in the Book of Life of the Lamb slain from the foundation of the world."

The saints who Satan makes war with are the people who become believers after the church is raptured out. Their names are added to the Book of Life. Satan is given power over all the tribes, tongues and nations of the world. The elect will not worship the beast therefore they are objects of his wrath.

Revelation 13:9

> "If anyone has an ear, let him hear."

This is a short verse but it is not to be taken lightly. The Lord is trying to get our attention. What I am telling you in this book is true and it is important.

> "Incline your ear, and come to Me: hear and your soul will live." (Isaiah 55:3)

If you reverse the scripture it means; if you don't hear, your soul shall die. That's pretty important. Jesus repeats over and over again throughout scripture, "he who has an ear, let him hear" (Revelation 2:7, 11, 17, 29; 3:6, 13, 22).

He is telling us to listen not only with our physical ears, but also with our spiritual ears because our mortal and immortal lives depend on it. Heaven or hell the choice is yours.

Revelation 13:10a

"He who leads into captivity shall go into captivity."

Satan leads people into captivity as well as the antichrist, false prophet, false teachers, cults and false religions. Eventually they themselves will be condemned to the Lake of Fire.

[SEE ALSO: REVELATION 19:20; 20:10-15]

Revelation 13:10b

"He who kills with the sword must be killed with the sword."

The antichrist and his followers will be killing believers and Jews during the tribulation by beheading with swords. When the Lord comes to take His vengeance out on the antichrist and his people, He will use the "rhomphaia" the "two-edged sword of the Lord" which is the Word of God. The enemy will be unable to stand as they hear the Word of God spoken directly out ot the mouth of Jesus.

[SEE ALSO: EPHESIANS 6:17B; HEBREWS 4:12; REVELATION 1:16; 19:21A]

When Jesus comes back as "King of kings and Lord of lords" riding His white horse and coming in the clouds, He speaks His word as His presence splits the darkness. The soldiers gathered at Armageddon will explode and their blood will pour out on the ground (Revelation 14:20).

Revelation 13:10c

"Here is the patience and the faith of the saints."

The persecution, suffering, torture and death of the saints will be more horrible than we can possibly imagine, but they will remain strong and faithful to the Lord.

Revelation 13:11-14

"Then I saw another beast coming up out of the earth, and he had two horns like a lamb and spoke like a dragon. And he exercises all the authority of the first beast in his presence, and causes the earth and those who dwell in it to worship the first beast, whose deadly wound was healed. He performs great signs, so that he even makes fire come down from heaven on the earth in the sight of men. And he deceives those who dwell on the earth by those signs which he was granted to do in the sight of the beast, telling those who dwell on the earth to make an image to the beast who was wounded by the sword and lived."

The first beast from Revelation 13:1 came out of the *sea*; the second beast comes out of the *earth*. Everything concerning the second beast is in the Book of Revelation and is not mentioned in any other book of the Bible.

In Greek the word for earth in this verse is "Ge", pronounced (ghay) meaning "world". It represents the people of the entire earth. This second beast is the false prophet representing the world's false religions. He is called the false prophet from the Greek word *"pseudo prophetes"* and is seen with the first beast (antichrist) and the dragon calling the armies of the world together to do battle with God Almighty in Revelation 16:13.

He appears after John's vision of the first beast and is called *another* beast. In Greek the word is *"allos"* which means "another of the same kind", showing both are demonic.

He had *"two horns like a lamb, and he spake as a dragon"*. The Lord is referred to in the Bible as the *"Lamb of God"*. The false prophet will try to imitate Jesus so he will look like a lamb, but with two horns. Lambs do not have horns and are meek and mild animals. Horns are symbols of authority in scripture. Jesus said in His Sermon on the Mount, *"Beware of false prophets, which come to you in sheep's clothing, but inwardly they are ravening wolves"* (Matthew 7:15). The false prophet will perform some minute signs but deceive many. The close relationship between these two world leaders is seen in that the false prophet will be given his power by the antichrist. The false prophet will be an executive of the antichrist.

[SEE ALSO: II THESSALONIANS 2:8-12]

After the antichrist comes into great influence the false prophet is not mentioned being apart from the antichrist. They will work in unison. Someone wanting to be the world dictator must be able to provide people with an outlet for their religious beliefs. The ecumenical church described in Revelation 17 will exert such power. It will seem like the church is dominating the antichrist while the antichrist is trying to solidify his political empire. Proof of this is revealed in Revelation17:3-7 where the woman (Papal Church) is riding on top (controlling) of the beast. After the first three and a half years of the tribulation the antichrist will no longer have any need for the woman (Papal Church). He will destroy her and set up his own form of worship. Satan will use the false prophet to unite all the false religions which will seem to please everyone. Satan is not against religion. He is against personal faith in Jesus Christ. The antichrist will be one of the chief spokesmen in the holy land in favor of the ecumenical power described in Revelation 17 until it no lon-

ger serves his purpose. He will then establish worship of himself.
[SEE ALSO: MATTHEW 4:8-10]

The antichrist will exalt himself and claim to be God. The false prophet is not a king and does not exalt himself but exalts the antichrist. The false prophet's relationship to the antichrist is similar to the Holy Spirits relationship to Christ. As the followers of Christ are sealed by the Holy Spirit until the day of redemption, the followers of antichrist shall be sealed by the false prophet until the Day of Judgment when they will be cast into the Lake of Fire. He will perform great signs and wonders. He will make fire come down from heaven in the sight of men. Jesus warned us in His gospels not to seek after signs and wonders.
[SEE ALSO: MATTHEW 12:38-40]

Even in many of today's Christian churches people look for some kind of sign. This pleases Satan because it takes there focus off Jesus. If non-believers see Christians looking for signs rather than seeking Jesus, then when Satan comes and does a few tricks, the people will be ready to flock to him. Many people are being attracted to what is called the New Age Movement, putting their hope in trinkets, stones, pictures, crystals, images, statues, mysticism, psychics, etc. and Satan loves it.

The false prophet will have supernatural powers in the presence of the beast and we are warned by Christ that if it would be possible, *"the very elect would be deceived"* (Matthew 24:24).

Revelation 13:14 says when the false prophet performs his miracles and wonders it is always *"in the presence of the beast"*. The Holy Spirit speaks and teaches us the things of God but the Holy Spirit does not need to be in the presence of the Father or Jesus to speak or teach the things of the Father and/or Jesus because they are one.

Revelation 13:15

"He was granted power to give breath to the image of the beast, that the image of the beast should both speak and cause as many as would not worship the image of the beast to be killed."

The false prophet will be given the power to make the image of the beast come to life. How he will cause it to speak and give it life scripture doesn't say but it will either be by supernatural powers, or possibly by using some kind of super computer. Considering today's technology it is not hard to believe this could be done. Those who refuse to worship the image will be killed.

[SEE ALSO: DANIEL 9:27; 12:11; MATTHEW 24:15; REVELATION 20:4B]

Revelation 13:16-18

"And he causes all, both small and great, rich and poor, free and slave, to receive a mark on their right hand or on their foreheads, and that no one may buy or sell except one who has the mark or the name of the beast, or the number of his name. Here is wisdom. Let him who has understanding calculate the number of the beast, for it is the number of a man: His number is 666."

It will not matter who you are or where you fit in society, either you receive the mark of the beast or you will hide and scavenge for your survival in the hopes that you will not be caught and killed.

Revelation 13:17 is absolutely clear. If you want to buy or sell anything, hold a job, own a house, a car, etc. you will have to have at least one of three things:

1. His *mark* in your right hand or forehead
2. The *name* of the beast in your right hand or forehead
3. The *number* of his name in your right hand or forehead

Over the years there has been much speculation about the *number of his name* identifying who the antichrist will be but scripture tells us it will not be known until the great tribulation is about to start and the *son of perdition* is revealed.

[SEE ALSO: II THESSALONIANS 2:3&4]

Many wonder why the mark of the beast will be "666". The number of man is 6; it stops short of the perfect or sacred number 7.

Man was created on the sixth day.

[SEE ALSO: GENESIS 1:26&27&31]

Various people have been declared to be the antichrist throughout history. Names have been translated into Greek, with a numerical value for each letter of the alphabet and the numbers of the person's name added up to get the total value of 666.

One must wonder if some practices of contemporary technology are precursors to the mark of the beast. Veterinarians put a chip under the skin of animals to keep track of them and their history.

AT&T has developed a chip to be used on human beings small enough so the chip can fit inside a common needle used for vaccinations. It can be injected into a persons right hand (oddly enough the chip will not work in the left hand) with your name, address, all your medical and any other history on it. A person can than be tracked by satellite. The government is trying to pass a law which would make it mandatory for all new born babies to get implanted with this chip under the guise of "if your baby is ever kidnapped or lost" law enforcement will be able to track them. The history of the child could be added to the chip as the person grows.

CHAPTER 14

In this chapter we are back into a "parenthetical" type passage. It explains what is about to happen between the blowing of the seventh trumpet and the end of the seven year tribulation. Keep in mind the events are not necessarily in sequence within the parenthetical verses.

Revelation 14:1a

> "Then I looked, and behold, a Lamb standing on Mount Zion."

John sees Jesus as the Lamb standing on Mount Zion in the New Jerusalem which presently is in heaven.

[SEE ALSO: ISAIAH 53:7B; JOHN 1:29&36; HEBREWS 12:22; I PETER 1:19; REVELATION 5:6A]

Revelation 14:1b

> "With Him one hundred and forty-four thousand, having His Father's name written on their foreheads."

The 144,000 are from the 12 tribes of Israel who preached throughout the earth during the tribulation (Revelation 7:3-8). Scripture does not reveal how the 144,000 got from earth to the New Jerusalem, only that they were redeemed.

Revelation 14:2

> "And I heard a voice from heaven, like the voice of many waters, and like the voice of loud thunder. And I heard the sound of harpists playing their harps."

What the voice says we are not told, but we know the voice is the LORD'S.

[SEE ALSO: EXODUS 19:17-19, 20:19; JOB 37:4&5, 40:9; PSALMS 29:3-5&7-9; REVELATION 1:15]

John says he hears *"harpists playing their harps."* Revelation 15:2b reveals these harpists are: *"Them that had gotten the victory over the beast, and over his image, and over his mark, and over the number of his name, standing on the sea of glass, having the harps of God."*

The martyrs are no longer under the sea of glass but standing on top of it going through their fiery baptism. They are no longer at Christ's feet but on the same level with Christ and His church, standing above the third heaven.

Revelation 14:3

> "And they sang as it were a new song before the throne, before the four living creatures, and the elders; and no one could learn that song except the hundred and forty-four thousand who were redeemed from the earth."

The 144,000 Israelites standing before the throne of God and before the church are taught a song only they can sing. Not even the Church is able to learn this song.

Revelation 14:4a

> "These are the ones who were not defiled with women, for they are virgins. These are the ones who follow the Lamb

wherever He goes. These were redeemed from among men."

This verse reveals why this song could only be learned by the 144,000 martyrs.

They kept themselves clean from all women; they were virgins in the truest sense. God set these 144,000 apart as His first fruits before they were even born.

Revelation 14:4b

"Being the first fruits unto God and to the Lamb."

They are the first fruits of the restored nation of Israel, not of the church.

"Israel was holiness to the LORD, the first fruits of His increase. All that devour him will offend; disaster will come upon them, 'says the LORD.'" (Jeremiah 2:3)

Revelation 14:5

"And in their mouth was found no guile, for they are without fault before the throne of God."

They are not only sexually pure but morally pure. They are pure in mouth which means they use no foul or vile language. They don't talk behind people's backs, degrade or verbally abuse people. They are pure in mind, spirit, heart, body and soul.

"The remnant of Israel shall not do iniquity, nor speak lies, neither shall a deceitful tongue be found in their mouth."
Zephaniah 3:13

[SEE ALSO: PSALMS 32:2]

Somewhere on earth today there may very well be the 144,000 Israelites walking around who fulfill this scripture. They are so pure even through the great tribulation, with the beast, false prophet and antichrist hunting them down, God says of them *"They are without fault before His throne"*. What an honor.

Revelation 14:6

> *"Then I saw another angel flying in the midst of heaven, having the everlasting gospel to preach to those who dwell on the earth-to every nation, tribe, tongue, and people."*

John sees an angel preaching the gospel which in all history has only been done by man, never by an angel. It is the only time an angel is commissioned to preach the gospel. This shows the seriousness of the situation of what is about to happen on earth. This angel is flying throughout the earth so everybody left has a chance to hear the gospel and no one from the tribulation will be able to stand before God and say "I never heard the truth". God in His loving kindness and mercy is still giving people a chance to turn to Him.

Is the *everlasting gospel* a different gospel from what we preach today? Is it a different gospel from what the apostles preached 2,000 years ago? Absolutely not, there are several terms used to describe the gospel in the Scriptures but only one gospel.

> *"But even if we, or an angel from heaven, preach any other gospel to you than what we have preached to you, let him be accursed. As we have said before, so now I say again, if anyone preaches any other gospel to you than what you have received, let him be accursed."* (Galatians 1:8&9)

[SEE ALSO: MATTHEW 24:14; EPHESIANS 6:15]

This angel will be warning the people to fear God instead of the antichrist; to give glory to God instead of the antichrist.

> *"And this gospel of the kingdom will be preached in all the world as a witness to all the nations, and then the end will come." (Matthew 24:14)*

The angel's announcement will bring into play the darkest days mankind has ever seen, or will ever see again.

Revelation 14:7

> *"Saying with a loud voice, "Fear God and give glory to Him, for the hour of His judgment has come; and worship Him who made heaven and earth, the sea and springs of water."*

The angel is announcing to all the earth the time is here. The hour has come, this is your last chance to acknowledge Jesus Christ as Lord and Savior and be rescued from what is about to happen.

Satan brainwashes people into believing things like "evolution" and the "big bang theory". Man has rejected God as the Creator and has tried to change the word of God into a lie. They have worshipped the *"creature"* instead of the *"Creator"* (Romans 1:25). Jesus Christ is the Creator of everything (John 1:1-3).

Before this devastating judgment falls upon the earth our compassionate, loving, merciful God gives people yet another chance to turn from their wickedness. The Book of Revelation teaches us anytime there is a major judgment about to happen God calls out to the people by way of messengers and warnings upon the earth. God has repeatedly warned the people in the end times. He sent the 144,000 witnesses, he empowered two witnesses supernaturally and he sent numerous signs in the heavens and catastrophes on the earth. Now an angel is sent to preach the everlasting gospel to those whose hearts are still hard.

Revelation 14:8

> "And another angel followed, saying, "Babylon is fallen, is fallen, that great city, because she has made all nations drink of the wine of the wrath of her fornication."

Revelation 17&18 are given over entirely to discussing Babylon in great detail. This is the first time Babylon is mentioned in this book. It is a preliminary announcement to the final overthrow of the city and of a religious system known as Babylon.

Babylon is first mentioned in Genesis 10&11. It was a city founded by a rebel named Nimrod. Babylon grew into a great Gentile world power which eventually would one day abuse all the nations of the world.

Babylon in Hebrew is "Babel" (baw-bel) which means "confusion". In Greek it is "Babylon" (bab-oo-lone) and means "tyranny". In the Old Testament it was the capital of Chaldea (modern day Iraq).

The name Babylon has several different meanings:

1. The city of Babylon located in present day Iraq
2. A false religious system
3. Vatican City in Rome
4. A name against Jerusalem
5. The country of Iraq

During the tribulation Satan will use the city of Babylon as the center of activity.

Scripture refers to two Babylon's in the book of Revelation and both are called "Babylon the Great". Both Babylon's will be destroyed because they both caused mankind to sin and we need to be careful not to confuse the two. The differences between the two Babylon's are explained in chapters 17 & 18.

Revelation 14:9-10

"Then a third angel followed them, saying with a loud voice, "If anyone worships the beast and his image, and receive his mark on his forehead or on his hand, he himself shall also drink of the wine of the wrath of God, which is poured out full strength into the cup of His indignation. And he shall be tormented with fire and brimstone in the presence of the holy angels and in the presence of the Lamb."

The choices are clear. People will worship the beast and be damned by God or worship God and be damned by the beast. There is no middle ground. Those who take the mark of the beast will be void of conscience and fear of God. They will be possessed and controlled by demon forces because they have relinquished their soul to the devil.

God continues to show His love, patience and long suffering by sending yet a third angel to warn mankind of the consequences they endure if they receive the mark of the beast. Once a person receives the mark *there is no turning back.*

Revelation 15:1 reveals the wrath of God mentioned in Revelation 14:10 and is completed with the pouring out of the seven last plagues; *"And I saw another sign in heaven, great and marvelous, seven angels having the seven last plagues; for in them is filled up the wrath of God".* As if the seven last plagues will not be enough punishment, Revelation 14:10b says: *"And he shall be tormented with fire and brimstone in the presence of His holy angels, and in the presence of the Lamb."*

Jesus warns us many times in the gospels about hell, but people didn't listen then nor do they listen now. Many today believe hell doesn't exist. How many times have you heard someone say "this is hell on earth", or, "my life is a living hell". Or they make a joke of it saying something like "well, I'll see you in hell and we can party". Hell is not a place of fun and games but a real place of eternal torment.

> "Therefore Sheol (Hell) has enlarged itself and opened its mouth beyond measure; their glory and their multitude and their pomp, and he who is jubilant, shall descend into it." (Isaiah 5:14)

[SEE ALSO: PSALMS 9:17; PROVERBS 15:24; MATTHEW 5:22C; 8:12; 18:9B]

There are too many scriptures to mention here which reveal hell as a real place of darkness, bitterness, weeping and gnashing of teeth.

Revelation 14:11

> "And the smoke of their torment ascends forever and ever; and they have no rest day or night, who worship the beast and his image, and whoever receives the mark of his name."

> "For it is the day of the LORD'S vengeance, the year of recompense for the cause of Zion its streams shall be turned into pitch, and its dust into brimstone; its land shall become burning pitch. It shall not be quenched night or day; its smoke shall ascend forever. From generation to generation it shall lay waste; no one shall pass through it forever and ever." (Isaiah 34:8-10)

In Revelation 21:1-8 God promises there will be no more tears or sorrow because all former things will be wiped away. The flames of hell will continue to punish the unsaved but we will either not be aware of it or because we will be in our perfected state will realize this is the just consequence for unbelievers.

Revelation 14:12

> *"Here is the patience of the saints; here are those who keep the commandments of God and the faith of Jesus."*

John is talking again about the last three and a half years of the great tribulation. All those who refuse the mark of the beast will be blessed by God although they will have to die a horrible death. Why will the saints need patience? Because those who refuse to worship the beast and don't accept his mark will be beaten, persecuted, tortured and killed. It will take strength and unimaginable faith to trust the Lord at this time. Those who know the truth will know it is better to suffer and die a martyr's death, than to live in luxury with the antichrist for three and a half years only to burn and be tormented in the Lake of Fire for all eternity.

How fortunate we are in this present day and age to have the opportunity to avoid all this because we can be saved by *"the grace of our Lord and Savior Jesus Christ"*. In the United States of America founded on Biblical principals and the belief in Jesus Christ we can still worship Him freely and not worry about being killed for our beliefs, at least not yet.

Revelation 14:13

> *"Then I heard a voice from heaven saying to me, "Write: 'Blessed are the dead who die in the Lord from now on.'"*
> *"Yes," says the Spirit, "that they may rest from their labors, and their works follow them."*

These are two quotes directly from the Holy Spirit who is called a teacher and a comforter.
[SEE ALSO: JOHN 14:16, 17&26]

One of the main themes of scripture apparent in Revelation is that our present day sufferings, trials, hardships and tribulations are inconsequential compared to the eternal blessings prepared for those who love the Lord.

Revelation 14:14

> "And I looked, and behold, a white cloud, and on the cloud sat one like the Son of Man, having on His head a golden crown, and in His hand a sharp sickle."

John is awestruck when he sees this cloud. It is so white because it is carrying our Lord and Savior, Jesus Christ.

> "Behold, the LORD rides on a swift cloud." (Isaiah 19:1b)

> "And Jesus said, 'I am: and ye shall see the Son of Man sitting on the right hand of power, and coming in the clouds of heaven.'" (Mark 14:62)

[SEE ALSO: PSALMS 104:3B; MATTHEW 24:30; 26:64B; MARK 13:26; I THESSALONIANS 4:17]

Some people believe when they read verse 14 this is an angel because of Revelation 14:15-17. But when you compare the wording of the scriptures, you can see the difference: Revelation 14:14 says: "one like the Son of Man"; where Revelation 14:17 specifically states "an angel".

Nowhere in the Bible do you ever see angels wearing crowns. After the rapture the saints (which are what believers are called) will receive up to five different types of crowns, depending upon the works they did on earth. Scripture says we will then cast them back at the feet of Jesus because we will know without Him we never would have earned them in the first place. (Revelation 4:4, 10&11)

In Greek, the word used here for *crowns* is "stephanos" and means "a wreathe made of gold."

The sharp sickle in Christ's hand has a different purpose from the sickle in the angel's hand of Revelation 14:17.

The word "sickle" in Greek is *drepanon* and means "a gathering hook".

Revelation 14:15

> "And another angel came out of the temple, crying with a loud voice to Him who sat on the cloud, "Thrust in Your sickle and reap, for the time has come for you to reap, for the harvest of the earth is ripe."

This angel is the fourth angel since Revelation 14:6 and comes out of the temple. Scripture doesn't reveal where the first three were when they were called to their tasks, but their mission was different from this fourth angel.

The first three angels are "messengers", each one delivering a specific message from God to the people on earth. This fourth angel comes directly from the "Holy of Holies" and is delivering an order to Jesus from the Father. Unlike the first three angels who were *speaking* with a loud voice; this fourth angel comes out of the temple *crying* with a loud voice.

Revelation 14:16

> "So He who sat on the cloud thrust in His sickle on the earth, and the earth was reaped."

Jesus is purging out the enemies of the nation of Israel by separating the "wheat from the tares", and the "sheep (nations) from the goat (nations)".

[SEE ALSO: ISAIAH 59:18&19; JEREMIAH 46:10; II THESSALONIANS 1:7-10]

Revelation 14:17

> "Then another angel came out of the temple which is in heaven, he also having a sharp sickle."

This angel is helping Jesus cast the unbelievers and the armies at Armageddon into the great wine press of the wrath of God. Only Christ has the right to judge the righteous from the unrighteous because Jesus is the one who died for us. Now that He has separated them, the angel helps cast the unbelievers into everlasting punishment.

> "Let the nations be wakened, and come up to the Valley of Jehoshaphat; for there I will sit to judge all the surrounding nations. Put in the sickle, for the harvest is ripe. Come, go down; for the winepress is full, the vats overflow-for their wickedness is great. Multitudes, multitudes in the valley of decision! For the Day of the LORD is near in the valley of decision." (Joel 3:12-14)

Revelation 14:18

> "And another angel came out from the altar, who had power over fire, and he cried with a loud cry to him who had the sharp sickle, saying, "Thrust in your sharp sickle and gather the clusters of the vine of the earth, for her grapes are fully ripe."

This angel, seen in the Old and New Testament is a Seraphim and comes from the altar, not from the temple. (Isaiah 6:6)

Revelation 14:19&20

> "So the angel thrust his sickle into the earth and gathered the vine of the earth, and threw it into the great winepress of the wrath of God. And the winepress was trampled outside the city, and blood came out of the winepress, up to the horses' bridles, for one thousand six hundred furlongs."

This event will take place outside the holy city of Jerusalem in the Valley of Meddago (Armageddon).
[SEE ALSO: REVELATION 16:16]

The enemies of Israel and God will be gathered here for the purpose of being destroyed by God and cast into hell. Blood will flow.
[SEE ALSO: ISAIAH 34:1-10; 63:1-4; EZEKIEL 38&39; ZECHARIAH 14; REVELATION 19:15-21]

The Bible gives reference of a furlong being one ninth of a mile. One ninth of a mile divided into 1,600 furlongs equals 177.77 miles. A bridal depth of a horse is approximately 4 feet high so there will be a *lake of blood* 177.77 square miles by 4 feet deep.

The armies of the world will be gathered against Israel which is a spec of land about the size of the state of New Jersey. They will have her surrounded in the Valley of Meddago with armies numbering well over 200,000,000 in the hope of finally eliminating the Jewish race. But God is on Israel's side and the armies of the world will be annihilated by Him. It will take Israel seven months to bury all the dead and Israel will finally inherit their Promised Land.
[SEE ALSO: EZEKIEL 39:12-16]

CHAPTER 15

Revelation 15:1

> *"Then I saw another sign in heaven, great and marvelous: seven angels having the seven last plagues, for in them the wrath of God is complete."*

The word *sign* in Greek is "semeion" meaning a sign, wonder, or symbol. In this instance it means wonder.

Chapter 15 reveals three important things:

1. It includes the events of chapters 10 through 15 regarding the visions in heaven and conditions on the earth up to the middle of the seven year tribulation.
2. It serves as an introduction to the last three and a half years of the great tribulation.
3. It reveals important truths concerning the wrath of God.

John witnessed two signs in Revelation 12:1&3 and now he sees another sign that is *"great and marvelous"*, revealing this is the most significant sign yet.

In the New Testament written in the Greek language the above phrase reads like this: *"Having the seven plagues, the last ones"*. After these last seven plagues it is the end of the age, not the world. The scroll has reached its end.

As the scroll unrolled it revealed seven *sealed* judgments *(Chapters 5, 6, &8)*; seven *trumpet* judgments *(Chapters 8, 9, & 11)* and now seven *bowl* judgments which will be poured out on the antichrist, beast, false prophet and their followers.

The seven angels (seven redeemed saints) are receiving their orders directly from God out of the Holy of Holies. God's patience and long suffering with mankind throughout the last 6,000 years has come to an end. The wrath is poured out on those who have rejected Jesus Christ throughout the ages and persecuted His church.

John does not see seven literal angels; but seven of his brethren in their glorified bodies going out to deliver the seven last plagues. Revelation 2&3 reveals that man can also be referred to as angels. The Greek word used here for angels is *aggelos* and means *messenger*, and *to bring tidings*. Who better to deliver the wrath of God on those who murdered the saints than the saints themselves.

Compare the following verses:

Revelation 17:1 "Then one of the seven angels who had the seven bowls came and talked with me, saying to me, 'Come, I will show you the judgment of the great harlot who sits on many waters.'"

> *"Then one of the seven angels who had the seven bowls filled with the seven last plagues came to me and talked with me, saying, 'Come, I will show you the bride, the Lamb's wife."(Revelation 21:9)*

In Revelation 19:10 read what the "angel" from Revelation 17 says to John: "And I (John) fell at his feet to worship him. But he said to me, 'See that you do not do that! I am your fellow servant, and of your brethren who have the testimony of Jesus. Worship God! For the testimony of Jesus is the spirit of prophesy." This is one of John's brothers in the Lord, a fellow servant, a converted Jew.

> *"And I said to him, "Sir, you know." So he said to me, "These are the ones who come out of the great tribulation, and washed their robes and made them white in the blood of the Lamb. Therefore they are before the throne of God, and serve Him day and night in His temple." (Revelation 7:14&15)*

The only one allowed in the earthly temple's Holy of Holies, was the high priest dressed in white robes with a golden girdle. The seven angels with the seven last plagues come from the temple dressed in white robes and golden girdles. This shows they minister to God in a priestly manner just as the priests ministered within the temple in the Old Testament.

[SEE ALSO: EXODUS 39:27-29; LEVITICUS 16:4]

Jesus is also described as wearing a white linen robe with a golden girdle and He is our High Priest of the order of Melchizedek.

[SEE ALSO: GENESIS 14:18-20; PSALMS 110:4; HEBREWS 5:6&8-10; 7:1-27]

The seven last plagues are reserved for the antichrist, his followers and the destruction of Babylon (Iraq, Iran & part of Afghanistan.)

Revelation 15:2

> *"And I saw something like a sea of glass mingled with fire, and those who have the victory over the beast, over his image and over his mark and over the number of his name, standing on the sea of glass, having harps of God."*

The only other place in the Bible the sea of glass is mentioned is in Revelation 4:6. It was smooth as glass with no one on it, but now it is mingled with fire and the martyrs from the great tribulation are standing on it. This is their baptism (purifying, or cleansing).

During the period of grace, we are saved by grace. At the time we decide to repent of our sinful ways and live our lives for Jesus we receive the infilling of the Holy Spirit which is our spiritual baptism (baptism by fire) just like the apostles received on the day of Pentecost.

[SEE ALSO: MATTHEW 3:11; ACTS 2:1-4]

The apostles had their water baptism at the Jordan River by John the Baptist. Christ did not have to be baptized but He did it as an outward show of obedience to His Father just as Christians choose to be baptized as an outward sign to the world that we are followers of Jesus Christ. These martyrs receive their fiery baptism on the sea of glass before the throne of God purified by the refiner's fire.

The word *refiner* in Hebrew is "tsaraph" *(tsaw-raf)* meaning to *make pure* or *purge away*.

[SEE ALSO: ISAIAH 1:25; ZECHARIAH 13:9; MALACHI 3:2&3]

Revelation 15:3&4

> "And they sing the song of Moses, the servant of God, and the song of the Lamb, saying: "Great and marvelous are Your works, Lord God Almighty! Just and true are Your ways, O King of the saints! Who shall not fear You, O Lord, and glorify Your name? For You alone are holy. For all nations shall come and worship before You, for Your judgments have been manifested."

The martyrs are singing the *song of Moses* found in Deuteronomy 32:1-44 and the *song of the Lamb* found in Revelation 15:3b & 4. These redeemed are not to be confused with the 144,000 in Revelation 14 who have harps. The 144,000 sing a *new song* which no one else can learn.

Revelation 15:5

> "After these things I looked, and behold, the temple of the tabernacle of the testimony in heaven was opened."

John sees the Holy of Holies opening before him.

Revelation 15:6-8a

> "And out of the temple came the seven angels having the seven plagues, clothed in pure bright linen, and having their chests girded with golden bands. Then one of the four living creatures gave to the seven angel's seven golden bowls full of the wrath of God who lives forever and ever. The temple was filled with smoke from the glory of God and from His power,"

As the living creature hands over the bowls John sees the temple filled with the glory of God and His power.

When the tabernacle was finished by Moses and the temple was completed by King Solomon, there was a cloud, but no smoke.

> "So that the priests could not stand to minister by reason of the cloud: for the glory of the LORD had filled the house of God." (II Chronicles 5:14)

[SEE ALSO: EXODUS 40:34&35; I KINGS 8:10&11]

But in Exodus 19:18 "And Mount Sinai was altogether on a smoke, because the LORD descended upon it in fire: and the smoke thereof ascended as the smoke of a furnace, and the whole mount quaked greatly."

There is smoke when there is judgment, but there is the cloud when there is grace.

The temple in heaven is an actual temple. Moses tabernacle and Solomon's temple were patterned after the heavenly temple.

[SEE ALSO: EXODUS 25:9&40; I CHRONICLES 28:11&12, 19; HEBREWS 8:5]

Revelation 15:8b

> "And no one was able to enter the temple till the seven plagues of the seven angels were completed."

Revelation Brought Down to Earth

Once these angels are handed the seven golden bowls filled with the wrath of God no man will have access to the presence of God while His wrath is being poured out upon the earth because He will not be dealing with man in grace and mercy, but with judgment and wrath.

CHAPTER 16

Revelation 16:1

> *"Then I heard a loud voice from the temple saying to the seven angels, "Go and pour out the bowls of the wrath of God on the earth."*

These last seven judgments constitute what Jesus referred to in Matthew 24:21 as the "Great Tribulation", the last 42 months of the seven year tribulation period *"For than shall be great tribulation, such as was not since the beginning of the world to this time, no, nor ever shall be."*

The destruction will be greater than the flood of Noah, Sodom and Gomorrah during Lot's time and the destruction of Egypt during the time of Moses combined together.

Revelation 16:2

> *"So the first angel went and poured out his bowl upon the earth, and a foul and loathsome sore came upon the men who had the mark of the beast and those who worshiped his image."*

These judgments are not figurative. Four of the judgments happened previously in Moses time. They are repetitions of the plagues of Egypt.

> *"Then the LORD said to Moses and Aaron, "Take handfuls of soot from a furnace and have Moses toss it into the air in the presence of Pharaoh. It will become fine dust over the whole land of Egypt, and festering boils will break out on men and animals throughout the land." (Exodus 9:8&9) (NIV)*

Just as the plagues fell upon the Egyptian people and their animals but did not harm the Israelites or their animals in Moses' time, the same will happen in the end time. The sores will inflict only those who worship the beast. There will be no doubt these plagues are from God. When God sent the plagues of boils upon the Egyptians, it hardened their hearts toward God. The pouring out of the bowls will have the same effect on the followers of the antichrist. These seven plagues pour out successively *(Revelation 16:10&11)*, unlike the plagues of Egypt where one plague stopped before another began *(Exodus 7-11)*.

Revelation 16:3

> *"Then the second angel poured out his bowl on the sea, and it became blood as of a dead man; and every living creature in the sea died."*

The first bowl poured out on the earth directly affected man. This second bowl affects all the oceans and seas of the earth.

The word ocean is not found in the Bible. Genesis 1:10a says *"And God called the dry land earth; and the gathering together of the waters He called Seas."* This bowl changes the oceans and seas into thick, sluggish, clotty blood which will kill every living creature in them. Imagine how this will smell. Commerce will be destroyed. Fishermen, restaurants and markets will be affected by this. Ships of all kinds including cruise ships and ocean liners will be stuck in the midst of all this death and decay and those on board will die.

Chapter 16

In Revelation 8&9 when the second *trumpet* angel sounds, one third of the seas become as blood and one third of the creatures in the sea die. It was a warning from God which people chose to ignore; but now there are no more warnings.

Revelation 16:4-7

> *"Then the third angel poured out his bowl on the rivers and springs of water, and they became blood. And I heard the angel of the waters saying: 'You are righteous, O Lord, the One who is and who was and who is to be, because you have judged these things, for they have shed the blood of saints and prophets, and You have given them blood to drink. For it is their just due.' And I heard another from the altar saying, 'Even so, Lord God Almighty, true and righteous are Your judgments.'"*

All the fresh water lakes, rivers and streams are turned to blood. Drinking water is gone. Everything living in the fresh water dies. A similar thing happened on a much smaller scale in Egypt to Pharaoh and his people:

> *"Thus says the LORD: 'By this you shall know that I am the LORD. Behold, I will strike the waters which are in the river with the rod that is in My hand, and they shall be turned to blood. And the fish that are in the river shall die, the river shall stink, and the Egyptians will loathe drinking the water of the river.'"* (Exodus 7: 17&18)

God has an angel in charge of the waters of the earth. This angel verifies what God has done to the water was the right and just thing to do in retribution for all the innocent blood of the saints and martyrs over the centuries which has been shed. I find it interesting the angel in charge of the waters takes time to verify God

and His deity. Another angel from the altar in Revelation 16:7 confirms what the angel of the waters says by stating *"Even so, Lord God Almighty, true and righteous are Thy judgments."*
[SEE ALSO: MATTHEW 18:16; II CORINTHIANS 13:1]

There is a parallel again between the third trumpet angel and the third bowl angel. In Revelation 8:10&11 when the third angel sounds the trumpet, one third of all the fresh water becomes blood and is unusable, but when the third angel pours out his bowl all the fresh water becomes blood and is unusable.

Revelation 16:8&9

> *"Then the fourth angel poured out his bowl on the sun, and power was given to him to scorch men with fire. And men were scorched with great heat, and they blasphemed the name of God who has power over these plagues; and they did not repent and give Him glory."*

In Revelation 8:12&13 one third of the sun was wiped out and one third of the moon and stars were blocked out which reduced the 24 hour day to a 16 hour day. In the above verse when the angel pours out the bowl upon the sun, *power is given unto it*. In other words, the heat radiating from the sun will be greatly intensified so that even though there is only 8 hours of daylight the sun will be strong enough to scorch men with fire. Things like pollution, volcanic ash, dust from the mountains and buildings crumbling and burning, fumes from forest fires, industrial waste and toxins, the destruction of the ozone layer and the ultra violet rays of the sun will all contribute to intensify this plague.

With the combination of these four plagues taking place at the same time one would think the people would repent and turn their hearts to God. Instead *"They repent not to give Him glory!"* Man's pride and stupidity will be his downfall just like it was Satan's.

> "Surely the day is coming; it will burn like a furnace all the arrogant and every evildoer will be stubble, and that day that is coming will set them on fire," says the LORD Almighty. Not a root or a branch will be left to them." (Malachi 4:1) (NIV)

[SEE ALSO: JOEL 1:15-20]

People will be begging to die but they will not ask God for help. They are going to get what they justly deserve – the wrath of God.

Revelation 16:10&11

> "Then the fifth angel poured out his bowl on the throne of the beast; and his kingdom became full of darkness; and they gnawed their tongues because of the pain. And they blasphemed the God of heaven because of their pains and their sores, and did not repent of their deeds."

The fifth bowl is aimed specifically at the throne of the beast and his kingdom. The throne of the beast at this time is in Jerusalem and his kingdom is the European Common Community (ECC) also known as the (Revived Roman Empire). It will be so dark people will chew their tongues to feel pain just to know they are still alive. How fitting this plague is reserved for the beast and his kingdom. It is a taste of what hell is like before they get there. This darkness corresponds to the ninth Egyptian plague but on a much grander scale.

> "For behold, the darkness shall cover the earth, and deep darkness the people." (Isaiah 60:2a)

Sin & evil will fill the people; there will be no light whatsoever in them.

[SEE ALSO: EXODUS 10:21-23; ISAIAH 13:9&10; JOEL 2:1&2; AMOS 5:18-20; NAHUM 1:8; ZEPHANIAH 1:15; MARK 13:24&25]

After all this, the people curse God.

Revelation 16:12-14

> *"Then the sixth angel poured out his bowl on the great River Euphrates, and its water was dried up, so that the way of the kings from the east might be prepared. And I saw three unclean spirits like frogs coming out of the mouth of the dragon, out of the mouth of the beast, and out of the mouth of the false prophet. For they are spirits of demons, performing signs, which go out to the kings of the earth and of the whole world, to gather them to the battle of that great day of God Almighty."*

The Euphrates River will be dried up and enables the armies of the Asian nations to cross the Euphrates River and gather with the armies of the world in the Valley of Megiddo for the ultimate purpose of destroying the Jews. This takes place at the very end of the great tribulation.

The Euphrates River is the eastern border of the land that God promised to Abraham and served as the eastern border of the Old Roman Empire. It is 1,800 miles long, the largest river in western Asia and has been a formidable boundary between the people of the East and those of the West for centuries.

When the sixth angel blew his trumpet in Revelation 9:14&15 four demonic angels which were bound in the River Euphrates were loosed for the purpose of gathering and leading the armies of 200,000,000 men to kill one third of the world's population. In Revelation 16:12 the four demons have accomplished their mission. They have prepared the 200,000,000 man army for the crossing of the Euphrates River on the *"Great Day of the LORD"*. This gigantic army will cross dry shod over the river which should be no surprise since the LORD dried up the Red Sea so that Israel could cross dry shod to escape out of the hands of Pharaoh and his army.

[SEE ALSO: EXODUS 14:16, 21, 22&29; 15:19]

Chapter 16

God also dried the Jordan River so that Israel could cross on dry ground into the land of Canaan.

"And the priests that bare the ark of the covenant of the LORD stood firm on dry ground in the midst of Jordan, and all the Israelites passed over on dry ground, until all the people were passed clean over Jordan." (Joshua 3:17) (KJV)

[SEE ALSO: ISAIAH 12:15 & 16]

The kings of the east are the Asian races: China, Japan, Korea, Vietnam, Thailand, Laos, and Taiwan. Some of these countries are already starting to make amends with each other and are forming alliances.

The meaning of the scripture is *"kings of the sun rising"*. It is interesting that a small island thousands of years after bible prophecy was written, calls itself Japan which means *rising sun*. Japan's national flag is the symbol of a rising sun and the Japanese kamikaze pilots of WW II wore a bandana with the symbol of the rising sun around their foreheads.

China's army today numbers over 200,000,000. When the other Asian nations join together they will easily have a marching army of 200,000,000. The Bible calls them kings and they will form a confederacy. The kings of the east are preparing to march against the antichrist and his army. Deceived by the lying tongues of demons, they will instead cross the Euphrates River and join forces with the antichrist in opposition to the coming of Jesus Christ and His army of saints and angels.

Three demons symbolized as frogs come out of the mouths of the dragon, the beast and the false prophet. Scripture tells us *"they are spirits of devils"*. These demons are going to have *"power to work miracles"* and therefore be able to deceive all for the specific purpose: *"To gather them to the battle of that great day of God Almighty"*.

> "The coming of the lawless one is according to the working of Satan, with all power, signs, and lying wonders, and with all unrighteous deception among those who perish, because they did not receive the love of the truth, that they might be saved. And for this reason God will send them strong delusion that they should believe the lie that they all may be condemned who did not believe the truth but had pleasure in unrighteousness." (II Thessalonians 2:9-12)(NKJV)

[SEE ALSO: I TIMOTHY 4:1&2]

These demons will cause the nations of the world to cooperate with the antichrist at Megiddo where the battle will be fought located approximately 15 miles southeast of modern day "Haifa" in Israel.

Revelation 16:15

> "Behold, I am coming as a thief. Blessed is he who watches, and keeps his garments, lest he walk naked and they see his shame."

The Lord is warning those remaining on the earth He will come swiftly and without warning.

> "For yourselves know perfectly that the Day of the Lord so cometh as a thief in the night." (I Thessalonians 5:2)

> "But the day of the Lord will come as a thief in the night, in which the heavens will pass away with a great noise, and the elements will melt with fervent heat; both the earth and the works that are in it will be burned up." (II Peter 3:10)

[SEE ALSO: MATTHEW 24:42-44; REVELATION 3:3]

Revelation 16:16

> "And they gathered them together to the place called in Hebrew, Armageddon."

This is a simple but profound statement. It is not the final battle but the name of the place where the battle at the end of the great tribulation will take place.

> *"While people are saying, "Peace and safety," destruction will come on them suddenly, as labor pains on a pregnant woman, and they will not escape. But you, brothers, are not in darkness so that this day should surprise you like a thief. You are all sons of the light and sons of the day. We do not belong to the night or to the darkness. So then let us not be like others, who are asleep, but let us be alert and self controlled. For those who sleep, sleep at night and those who get drunk, get drunk at night. But since we belong to the day, let us be self-controlled, putting on faith and love as a breastplate, and the hope of salvation as a helmet. For God did not appoint us to suffer wrath but to receive salvation through our Lord Jesus Christ. He died for us so that, whether we are awake or asleep, we may live together with Him. Therefore encourage one another and build each other up, just as in fact you are doing."(I Thessalonians 5:3-11) (NIV)*

[SEE ALSO: II THESSALONIANS 1:6-10]

Revelation 16:17-19

> *"Then the seventh angel poured out his bowl into the air, and a loud voice came out of the temple of heaven, from the throne, saying, "It is done!" And there were noises and thunderings and lightnings; and there was a great earthquake, such a mighty and great earthquake as had not occurred since men were on the earth. Now the great city was divided into three parts, and the cities of the nations fell. And great Babylon was remembered before God, to give her the cup of the wine of the fierceness of His wrath."*

The first bowl was directed upon the *earth*; the second bowl on the *sea*; the third bowl on the *rivers, lakes, streams* and *fountains*; the fourth bowl on the *sun*; the fifth bowl was directly on the *seat and kingdom of the beast*; the sixth bowl on the *Euphrates River* to dry it up and now the seventh bowl is poured out into the *air*. God demonstrates His power as creator by affecting everything He has created.

As soon as the seventh bowl is poured into the air, a great voice comes out of the temple from the throne of God saying, "It is done". Those words were heard before in John 19:30 when Jesus said "It is finished" and He bowed His head, and gave up His spirit."

Jesus fulfilled every scripture in the Old Testament that related to Him from His "birth of a virgin" to His "death on the cross". Now, He shouts out from the throne in heaven "It is done". He is letting everyone know in heaven and earth that every *"jot and tittle"* of the scriptures from the beginning (creation) to the end (the return of Jesus to the earth as King of kings and Lord of lords) has been completed.

> "And He said unto me: 'It is done. I am Alpha and Omega, the beginning and the end.'" (Revelation 21:6a)

The seventh bowl signifies the return of Jesus Christ to the earth. It is the last bowl of wrath and happens right at the very end of the great tribulation just as Christ and His saints are about to come back to the earth. The armies of the world are gathered at Megiddo and tiny Israel is surrounded by over a 200,000,000 man army. Satan deceived his followers into believing they will win. They have Israel surrounded with the biggest army ever put together in the history of mankind and believe they will finally accomplish what so many others failed to do - destroy every man, woman and child of Jewish descent. God's plan was to get Satan and all his followers in one spot to destroy them. Just as those bullets, rockets, bombs and missiles are about to fall on Israel to annihilate the Jews forever, thunder roars and lightning streaks through the sky. Mighty voices cry out throughout the heavens followed by an earthquake shaking the entire world.

> "But your enemies will become like fine dust, the ruthless hordes like blown chaff. Suddenly, in an instant, the LORD Almighty will come with thunder and earthquake and great noise, with wind storm and tempest and flames of a devouring fire. Then the hordes of all the nations that fight against Israel, that attack her and her fortress and besiege her, will be as it is with a dream, with a vision in the night-as when a hungry man dreams that he is eating, but he awakens, and his hunger remains; as when a thirsty man dreams that he is drinking, but he awakens faint, with his thirst unquenched. So will it be with the hordes of all the nations that fight against Mount Zion." (Isaiah 29:5-8)(NIV)

[SEE ALSO: EZEKIEL 38&39:1-21; JOEL 2:10&11]

Revelation 16:20

> "Then every island fled away, and the mountains were not found."

The combination of the earthquakes and enormous tidal waves will destroy all the islands and every mountain on earth will be leveled to dust. The face of the earth will be dramatically changed.

> "For in My jealousy and in the fire of My wrath have I spoken, Surely in that day there shall be a great shaking in the land of Israel; so that the fishes of the sea, and the fowls of the heaven, and the beasts of the field, and all creeping things that creep upon the earth, and all the men that are upon

> the face of the earth, shall shake at My presence, and the mountains shall be thrown down, and the steep places shall fall, and every wall shall fall to the ground." (Ezekiel 38:19&20)

Revelation 16:21

> "And great hail from heaven fell upon men, every hailstone about the weight of a talent. And men blasphemed God because of the plague of the hail, since that plague was exceedingly great."

Added to the earthquakes, tidal waves, thunder, lightning and great voices, is hail weighing more than one hundred pounds. After all this man still curses God instead of repenting. The great city Babylon, the capital of the world at that time will split into three parts.

> "Babylon is fallen, is fallen, that great city, because she made all nations drink of the wine of the wrath of her fornication" (Revelation 14:8)

> "And, behold, here cometh a chariot of men, with a couple of horsemen. And he answered and said, Babylon is fallen, is fallen; and all the graven images of her gods he hath broken unto the ground." (Isaiah 21:9)

[SEE ALSO: JEREMIAH 50&51]

CHAPTER 17

This is another *parenthetical* chapter.

Revelation 16 took us to the end of the great tribulation with the pouring out of the seventh bowl. Now, one of the angels will explain to John the things he has seen but does not understand. It is likely John's head is swimming from everything which has been revealed to him. He is a man from the first century A.D. being shown things which are not going to happen until the twenty-first century or later. Everything John has been shown so far is terrifying. He is unable to identify much of it. The angel is going to explain to John the "Great Whore the mystery woman" and the judgment which will befall her.

Earlier I warned not to confuse the Babylon's from chapter 17 and 18. Some differences which show two distinct Babylon's are:

1. The beast and the ten kings will give the illusion of being under the domination of the papal church (great whore) for the first three and a half years of the tribulation. The false prophet will gain control of the papal church, unite all the false religions on the earth (the true church is already in heaven) and turn control over to the antichrist at the beginning of the last three and a half years of the great tribulation. This is why the woman is riding on top (in control) of the beast during the first three and a half years *(Revelation 17:3-6)*: but the beast is alone and the woman is nowhere to be found in the last three and a half years of the great tribulation.

2. The woman and the beast are symbolic in Revelation 17, but in Revelation 18 it is an actual city.

3. In Revelation 17 the angel is talking directly to John, but in Revelation 18 John only hears a voice announcing certain facts *(Revelation 18:1,2,4,10,16,18&21)*.

4. In Revelation 17 only one angel is speaking, but in Revelation 18 both men and angels speak.

5. In Revelation 17 Babylon is called "the woman" and a "great whore" and John wonders with great admiration over her *(Revelation 17:7)*. In Revelation 18 because John is well acquainted with the City of Babylon (modern day Iraq/Iran) he has no such reaction.

6. There are no prophecies or warnings concerning the destruction of "Mystery Babylon" but there are many prophecies throughout the Bible regarding the destruction of the City of Babylon in the end times.

"Babylon, the jewel of kingdoms, the glory of the Babylonian's pride, will be overthrown by God like Sodom and Gomorrah. She will never be inhabited or lived in through all generations; no Arab will pitch his tent there, no shepherd will rest his flocks there." (Isaiah 13:19&20)(NIV)

[SEE ALSO: ISAIAH 14:4-7; 21:9; JEREMIAH 50:35-40; 51:6-9&24-58]

7. When "Mystery Babylon" is destroyed the beast and ten kings rejoice *(Revelation 17:16&17)*, but when the City of Babylon is destroyed the beast and ten kings mourn her destruction *(Revelation 18:9-19)*.

The angel is about to reveal to John one of the mysteries of God. The word mystery is not referring to something mysterious but to a *truth* that has not previously been shown to man.

Revelation 17:15

"And he said to me, "The waters which you saw, where the harlot sits, are peoples, multitudes, nations, and tongues.""

[SEE ALSO: JEREMIAH 51:12-14]

Through scripture the Lord slowly reveals who the "great harlot" is and what she represents.

"All because of the wanton lust of a harlot, alluring, the mistress of sorceries, who enslaved nations by her prostitution and peoples by her witchcraft. I am against you, declares the LORD Almighty. I will lift your skirts over your face. I will show the nations your nakedness and the kingdoms your shame." (Nahum 3:4&5) (NIV)

[SEE ALSO: REVELATION 19:2]

Revelation 17:5&6

"And on her forehead a name was written:
>   *MYSTERY,*
>   *BABYLON THE GREAT*
>   *THE MOTHER OF HARLOTS AND OF THE*
>   *ABOMINATIONS OF THE EARTH*

And I saw the woman, drunk with the blood of the saints and with the blood of the martyrs of Jesus. And when I saw her, I marveled with great amazement."

Revelation 17:9

"Here is the mind which has wisdom: The seven heads are seven mountains on which the woman sits."

The great whore sits on seven mountains. Revelation 17:18 is one of the most revealing clues as to who the great whore is: "And the *woman whom you saw is that great city which reigns over the kings of the earth."* There has only been one city which ever had power to rule, reign and influence entire nations; *Vatican City* in the heart of Rome which sits on *"seven mountains"*.

The Roman Papal Church in the end times is a false, worldwide apostate demonic run church, full of witchcraft and paganism. The true Christian Church made up from all races, peoples and nations is already with Jesus Christ in heaven.

[SEE ALSO: I THESSALONIANS 4:13-18; I CORINTHIANS 15:20-26; 51-58]

The word mystery is found in several books of the bible and its context usually refers in some way to either Christ's church, or Satan's false church.

> *"Even the mystery which hath been hid from ages and from generations, but now is made manifest to His saints: to whom God would make known what is the riches of the glory of this mystery among the Gentiles; which is Christ in you, the hope of glory."* (Colossians 1:26&27)

> *"Now to Him that is of power to establish you according to my gospel, and the preaching of Jesus Christ, according to the revelation of the mystery, which was kept secret since the world began, but now is made manifest, and by the scriptures of the prophets, according to the commandment of the everlasting God, made known to all nations for the obedience of faith."* (Romans 16:25&26)

[SEE ALSO: EPHESIANS 3:3-12; I CORINTHIANS 4:1]

This passage reveals the mystery of the church, Christ's bride was established since the world began, written of by the prophets over a thousand years before it happened, proving the scriptures are inspired by God, not by man.

Colossians 4:3 Paul tells us he was thrown in prison for speaking of the mystery of Christ *"Meanwhile praying also for us, that God* would open to us a door for the word, to speak the mystery of Christ, for which I am also in chains."

> "And without controversy great is the mystery of godliness: God was manifested in the flesh, justified in the Spirit, seen by angels, preached among the Gentiles, believed on in the world, received up in glory." (I Timothy 3:16)

[SEE ALSO: MARK 4:11; I CORINTHIANS 2:7&8; I TIMOTHY 3:8&9]

In Revelation 1:20 Jesus said: *"The mystery of the seven stars which you saw in My right hand, and the seven golden lampstands: The seven stars are the angels (leaders/messengers) of the seven churches, and the seven lampstands which you saw are the seven churches."*

Satan is the great imposter always trying to duplicate Christ. Satan tries to have his own mystery church. The name of Satan's church is *"Mystery Babylon the Great"*, the representation of all the false and pagan religions throughout the ages.

> "Don't let anyone deceive you in any way, for that day will not come until the rebellion occurs and the man of lawlessness is revealed, the man doomed to destruction. He will oppose and exalt himself over everything that is called God or is worshipped, so that he sets himself up in God's temple, proclaiming himself to be God." (II Thessalonians 2:3&4)

[SEE ALSO: I JOHN 4:2&3]

John was shown Christ's bride "New Jerusalem" as a city that represents total purity and goodness. Satan names his church "Babylon" after a city that represents total evil.

> "Then one of the seven angels who had the seven bowls filled with the seven last plagues came to me and talked with me, saying, "Come, I will show you the bride, the Lamb's wife. And he carried me away in the Spirit to a great and high mountain, and showed me the great city, the holy Jerusalem, descending out of heaven from God." (Revelation 21:9&10)

We need to look back in history approximately 4,000 years to the time just after the flood of Noah to understand where and how Mystery Babylon started, who its founder was and how it ties in with today's Roman Catholic Church. We look in the first book of the bible Genesis to explain a passage in the last book of the bible Revelation.

Nimrod (Nimrod-bar-cush) was a grandson of Ham, the unworthy son of Noah. Noah believed and trusted in God. He brought the revelation of the true God through the flood but Ham was caught up in the sins that caused the flood in the first place. Ham's name means "swarthy", "darkened" or "the sun burnt". The name indicates the state of a man's soul.

Ham begat a son named Cush, which means the *Black One* and he was the father of Nimrod. Nimrod became the apostate leader of his generation. Nimrod married *Semiramis the First*; founder of the Babylonian Mysteries and the first high-priestess of idolatry.

Babylon became the fountainhead of idolatry and the mother of every heathen and pagan religious system in the world. This pagan religion spread in various forms throughout the earth and is still with us today. It will have its fullest influence when Christ's church is raptured and the Holy Spirit departs.

Semiramis bore a son (Tammuz) whom she declared was miraculously conceived, so he was hailed as the promised deliverer. In the days of Israel's captivity the people were lured into this pagan religion. Israel started sacrificing their first born sons and daughters in fire to this pagan god.

[SEE ALSO: EZEKIEL 8:6-14; 16:20&21; 23:36-39]

Revelation 17:9-12

> "Here is the mind which has wisdom: The seven heads are seven mountains on which the woman sits. There are also

seven kings. Five have fallen, one is, and the other has not yet come. And when he comes, he must continue a short time. And the beast that was, and is not, is himself also the eighth, and is of the seven, and is going to perdition. And the ten horns which you saw are ten kings who have received no kingdom as yet, but they receive authority for one hour as kings with the beast."

The bible and history reveal that through time and wars *Mystery Babylon* blended together to become both the *Roman Empire* and the *Roman Catholic Church*.

The first of the seven kings (kingdoms) was EGYPT which originally held Israel in bondage. It was in Egypt where Israel suffered her first great oppression under Pharaoh for 400 years.
[SEE ALSO: GENESIS 15:13&14; EXODUS]

In the time of king Rehoboam, Judah was chastened by Egypt.
[SEE ALSO: I KINGS 14:25&26]

Egypt is to be a part of the antichrists kingdom in the last days.
[SEE ALSO: DANIEL 11:42&43]

Egypt will be part of the division of Greece that will be one of the ten kingdoms in the last days.

Egypt's downfall and destruction in the end times is referred to in Ezekiel 29-32.

The second of the seven kingdoms was ASSYRIA which took the ten tribes of Israel captive. Assyria had many relationships with Israel which is documented in the books of: II Kings 15-18, I & II Chronicles, Jeremiah, Hosea, Zephaniah, Zechariah. Assyria formed alliances with Judah against Israel. Because Assyria oppressed Israel, its downfall is prophesied.
[SEE ALSO: ISAIAH 10:24-27; 11:16; 14:25; 31:8&9; MICAH 5:5&6]

The remnant (believers) who are left of Egypt and Assyria after the tribulation will be blessed with Israel in the millennium.

[SEE ALSO: ISAIAH 19:23-25]

The third of the seven kingdoms, the *Head of Gold* in King Nebuchadnezzar's dream, is BABYLON (IRAQ, IRAN, and part of AFGHANISTAN). (Daniel 2:36-38)

Babylon was involved with Israel and Judah on various occasions in scripture.

[SEE ALSO: II KINGS 17:24, II CHRONICLES 33:11]

Babylon captured Judah and held her captive for seventy years.

[SEE ALSO: JEREMIAH 25:11-14]

Babylon is mentioned in seventeen books of the Bible and in numerous verses. *(II Kings; I&II Chronicles; Ezra; Nehemiah; Esther; Psalms; Isaiah; Jeremiah; Ezekiel; Daniel; Micah; Zechariah; Matthew; Acts; I Peter and Revelation)*

The fourth of the seven kingdoms, the *Chest of Silver* in King Nebuchadnezzar's dream is MEDO-PERSIA (King Cyrus & King Darius). Medo-Persia helped Babylon in the overthrow of Assyria and is mentioned directly and indirectly in several different chapters of the Book of Daniel. There are several different symbols used in scripture for Medo-Persia which is mentioned as being ruled by satanic princes.

[SEE ALSO: DANIEL 7:5, 8:3&4, 20;]

> *The angel Gabriel explained to Daniel why he was late in answering Daniel's prayers to the Lord "But the prince of the Persian kingdom resisted me twenty-one days. Then Michael, one of the chief princes, came to help me, because I was detained there with the king of Persia. Now I have come to explain to you what will happen to your people in the future, for the vision concerns a time yet to come."*

> "So he said, "Do you know why I have come to you? Soon I will return to fight against the prince of Persia, and when I go, the prince of Greece will come; but first I will tell you what is written in the Book of Truth. No one supports me against them except Michael, your prince."
> Daniel 10:13, 14, 20&21 (NIV)

Other activities regarding Medo-Persia, which conquered Babylon, are mentioned in the Book of Ezra.

The fifth of the seven kingdoms, the *Belly and Thighs of brass* in King Nebuchadnezzar's dream is GREECE (Alexander the Great).

This kingdom is symbolized as a "leopard with four heads".

> "After this I looked, and there was another, like a leopard, which had on its back four wings of a bird. The beast also had four heads, and dominion was given to it." (Daniel 7:6)

History and scripture reveal after the death of Alexander the Great his kingdom was divided into four divisions and given to his four generals.

Numerous scriptures relate to the antichrist coming out of the Grecian empire being revived under the Old Roman Empire in the end times during the great tribulation.

[SEE ALSO: DANIEL 7:6]

These five kingdoms are referred to as the five heads on the beast that fell before John's time. The antichrist will be of Grecian decent.

The sixth of the seven kingdoms, the *legs of iron and feet part iron and part clay* in King Nebuchadnezzar's dream, is ROME which was founded in 30 B.C. by Julius Caesar.

[SEE ALSO: DANIEL 2:40]

Rome is the kingdom symbolized on the beast as the "head that was" during Johns life time around 70 A.D. when Domitian was the ruler of Rome. At that time the Roman Empire was in control of the world and strong as iron. John was exiled to the Isle of Patmos off the coast of Greece, and General Titus marched into Jerusalem with the Roman army. During a four month siege General Titus destroyed the city and the temple leaving no stone on top of each other fulfilling the scriptures Mark 13:2; Luke 19:43&44. General Titus and his army killed over 1,000,000 Jews and took over 100,000 captives.

The kingdom of Rome in the end times is seen as dreadful, terrible and very strong, having ten horns (ten kingdoms under his control).

[SEE ALSO: DANIEL 7:7&8]

The Roman Empire was divided in 364A.D. into the eastern capital Rome and western capital Constantinople (the two legs of iron). As the result of the ecclesiastical separation it lost much of its life as a world power but it has never lost its religious existence or influence of the Greek and Roman Catholic Churches throughout the world. Roman law is still a strong controlling power in laws today. In this sense the Roman Empire has never ceased to exist or be destroyed.

The seventh kingdom against Israel will be the REVIVED ROMAN EMPIRE which is today's European Common Community. Under the leadership of the antichrist there will once again be a massive and severe persecution of Jews and Christians. The ten horns and ten toes of Daniel 2&7 correspond to the ten horns and ten kings of Revelation 12; 13&17 which Christ will destroy at His second coming.

The *beast* will be the eighth kingdom/king. The antichrist will be of Grecian and Jewish decent. He will rise to power and rule over the revived Roman Empire.

How Babylon became the Roman Catholic Church

How did Babylonian mysticism found in the Book of Genesis become the Roman Catholic Church of the twenty first century?

I believe Clarence Larkin; in his book *"Dispensational Truth"* explained it best.

Babel, or Babylon, was built by Nimrod and founded the Babylonian cult (Genesis 10:8-10). This system claimed to possess the highest wisdom to reveal the most divine secrets. Before a member could be initiated he had to confess his sins to the priest. The priest would then blackmail the person by threatening to reveal his sins to the public if the person tried to leave the cult, or reveal any of the cult's secrets. This is the origination of the sacrament of confession in the Roman Catholic Church. Once admitted into the order, men were no longer considered Babylonians, Assyrians or Egyptians but members of a mystical brotherhood over who was placed a high priest or Pontiff whose word was law.

City of Babylon

From the days of Nimrod *(Genesis 10:10)* Babylon grew in size and importance until it reached its greatest glory during the reign of King Nebuchadnezzar 604B.C.-562B.C.

It was an exact square of 15 miles surrounded by a brick wall that was 87 feet thick and 350 feet high. On the wall were 250 towers and the top of the wall was wide enough to allow six (6) chariots to drive along side each other. Outside the wall was a huge ditch surrounding the city that was filled with water fed from the Euphrates River. Inside the wall and not far from it was another wall, not much inferior, but narrower extending around the city.

Twenty five magnificent avenues, 150 feet wide ran across the city from north to south and the same number crossed them from east to west. The city was divided into two equal parts by the Euphrates River that flowed diagonally through it and whose banks within the city were walled up and pierced with brazen gates, with steps leading down to the river. At the end of the main avenues, on each side of the city, were gates, whose leaves of brass shone like "leaves of flame" as they were opened or closed in the rising or the setting of the sun.

The Euphrates River within the city was spanned by a bridge at each end of which there was a palace and these palaces were connected by passageways underneath the bed of the river in which at different points were located lavish banqueting rooms constructed entirely of brass.

Near one of these palaces stood the Tower of Babel consisting of eight (8) towers, each one being 75 feet high, rising one on top of the other with an outside winding stairway to its top. A pagan chapel on the top made up a combined height of six hundred sixty (660) feet.

This chapel contained the most expensive furniture of any place of worship in the world. Just one of the golden images, 45 feet high was valued at $17,500,000, and the whole of the sacred utensils were valued at $200,000,000.

Babylon also contained one of the Seven Ancient Wonders of the World, the famous "Hanging Gardens". These gardens were 400 square feet raised in terraces one above the other to the height of 350 feet and were climbed by stairways that were 10 feet wide. The top of each terrace was covered with large stones on which was laid a bed of rushes, then a thick layer of asphalt, next, two courses of brick cemented together and finally plates of lead to prevent leakage.

The garden was than covered with earth and planted with shrubbery and large trees. From a distance it had the appearance of a forest covered mountain, which was a remarkable sight in the flat Plains of the Euphrates. These gardens were built by King Nebuchadnezzar to please his wife who came from the mountainous country of Media, and by having these gardens was content with her surroundings.

Babylon is intimately connected with the history of Israel. A large part of the Books of Daniel and Jeremiah relate to Babylon. Babylon is also mentioned in 11 other books of the Old Testament and four in the New Testament.

Babylon has been conquered and destroyed many times throughout history. But it has never been as devastated as the Book of Revelation tells us it will be in the end times when God pours out His wrath upon it.

A detailed description of Babylon's destruction at the end of the great tribulation is found in Isaiah 13&14 and Jeremiah 50&51.

Babylon was captured in 541B.C. by Cyrus, king of the Medes and Darius, king of Persia. So quietly and quickly was the city captured on the night of King Belshazzar's feast that some inhabitants did not know till three days later that the king had been slain and the city captured (Daniel 5). There was no destruction of the physical City of Babylon at that time.

Twenty five years later in 516B.C. Babylon revolted against King Darius and after a fruitless siege of almost 20 months was finally taken by the use of strategy rather than actual combat.

About 478B.C, Xerxes, on his return from Greece, plundered but did not destroy the great Temple of Babylon.

In 331B.C. Alexander the Great approached Babylon which was once again so powerful that he made preparations for bringing his entire army into action in case it should offer resistance but the citizens threw open the gates and received him with great rejoicing!

After sacrificing to the god "Bel" or "Babel" he rebuilt the temple of that god and for weeks he kept 10,000 men employed in clearing away the ruins from the foundation intending to revive the glory of Babylon and make it his capital. But Alexander died of marsh fever and alcoholism at the age of 32 just one month shy of his 33rd birthday, so the task was never completed.

During the years that followed, Alexander's four generals fought over the control of Babylon. Babylon suffered much damage and finally came under the control of general Seleucus who built a capital for himself out of the remains. He renamed it Seleucia around 293B.C. By 25A.D. the city of Seleucia was almost deserted. Sometime between 25A.D. and 60A.D, the city was renamed Babylon. The Jews, left over from the captivity still resided their in large numbers and in 60A.D. the apostle Peter was working among them. It was from Babylon that Peter wrote his Epistle:

"The church that is at Babylon, elected together with you, salute you; and so does Marcus my son." (I Peter 5:13)

Around the middle of the 5th century A.D., Theodoret (a historian) says "Babylon is only inhabited by Jews and still had three Jewish Universities their". In the last year of the 5th century the "Babylonian Talmud" was issued and recognized authoritative by the Jews of the whole world.

In 917A.D. Ibu Hankel mentions Babylon as an insignificant village but still in existence.

In 1100A.D. Babylon grew again into a town of some importance because it was called the "Town of Two Mosques". Shortly after that it was enlarged and renamed: "Hillah" (rest).

In 1898A.D. Hillah contained about 10,000 people and was surrounded by fertile lands and abundant date groves stretched along the banks of the Euphrates.

In 2006A.D.it is known as "Al Hillah" located 56 miles south of present day Baghdad.

There are prophesies for Babylon which have yet to be fulfilled:

> "Look, here comes a man in a chariot with a team of horses. And he gives back the answer: 'Babylon has fallen, has fallen! All the images of its gods lie shattered on the ground!'" (Isaiah 21:9)(NIV)

> "No rock will be taken from you for a cornerstone, nor any stone for a foundation, for you will be desolate forever, declares the LORD." (Jeremiah 51:26)(NIV)

[ISAIAH 13:20; JEREMIAH 51:7-9&43]

Many towns and cities up to the present day have been built from the ruins of Babylon. Hillah was constructed entirely from the debris of Babylon and houses in present day Baghdad have Babylonian stamped bricks in them.

Isaiah tells of the time when the prophesies will be fulfilled:

> "Behold, the Day of the LORD comes, cruel with both wrath and fierce anger, to lay the land desolate; and He will destroy its sinners from it." (Isaiah 13:9)(NKJV)

The City of Babylon continued to be the seat of Satan until the fall of the Babylonian and Medo-Persian empires. Satan than moved his capital to Pergamum in Asia Minor. When Attalu, the Pontiff and king of Pergamum died in 133B.C. he bequeathed (willed) the headship of the Babylonian priesthood to Rome. When the Etruscans came to Italy from Lydia (the region of Pergamum) they brought with them the Babylonian religion and rites. They set up a new Pontiff to be the head of the priesthood.

Later, the Romans accepted the Pontiff as their civil ruler. Julius Caesar was made Pontiff of the Etruscan Order in 74B.C. In 63B.C.

he was made Supreme Pontiff of the Babylonian Order thus becoming heir to the rights and titles of Attalus, Pontiff of Pergamum, who had made Rome his heir. The first Roman Emperor (Julius Caesar) also became the head (Pontiff) of the Babylonian Priesthood and Rome the successor to Babylon.

The emperors of Rome continued to exercise the office of Supreme Pontiff until 376A.D. when Emperor Gration, who was a Christian, refused the office.

Damasus, the bishop of the Church of Rome was elected to the position. Damasus had been bishop for twelve years starting in 366A.D. through the influence of the Monks of Mt. Carmel, a college of Babylonian religion originally founded by the priests of Jezebel. In 378A.D. the head of the Babylonian Order became the ruler of the Roman Church thus Satan united Rome and Babylon into one religious system. Soon after Damasus was made Supreme Pontiff, the rites of Babylon were openly practiced. Worship of the Virgin Mary began in 381A.D. and all the outstanding festivals of the Roman Catholic Church are of Babylonian origin.

Revelation 17:4

> "The woman was arrayed in purple and scarlet, and adorned with gold and precious stones and pearls, having in her hand a golden cup full of abominations and the filthiness of her fornication."

Scarlet and purple are the colors of the Papacy. When a pope is installed into office he is required to wear scarlet colored clothes, a purple robe, a vest covered in pearls and a miter adorned with gold and precious stones.

After the believers are taken out of the world the false papal church will remain and the believers of all the pagan religions *"hav-*

ing the form of godliness, but denying the power thereof" (II Timothy 3:5) will join the false Papal Church and become a Universal Church under the leadership of the false prophet.

The Babylonian church of Revelation 17:4 can be easily mistaken for the City of Babylon (modern day Iraq) mentioned in Revelation 18:12&16 if the scriptures are not studied carefully. Both the woman and the beast are dressed in scarlet (symbol of royalty and ruler ship).

The woman is holding a golden chalice full of abominations of her fornications. She is drunk with the blood of the saints and martyrs of Jesus Christ.

> *"They will put you out of the synagogue: in fact, a time is coming when anyone who kills you will think he is offering a service to God." (John 16:2)(NIV)*

During the middle of the seven year tribulation the beast from the bottomless pit will take possession of the dead body of the leader of the E.C.C. and become the (8th king but is of the seventh) and the false prophet will relinquish control of the church, giving the antichrist world control both politically and religiously. He will take her wealth and treasure for himself and carry it back to the City of Babylon. The antichrist will become the center of worship and continue the slaughter of Jews and tribulation believers who refuse to follow the beast.

[SEE ALSO: ISAIAH 21:9; JEREMIAH 51:7-9; REVELATION 14:8]

The angel explains to John in Revelation 17:8-13 who the beast is, how he will come into being and how those not written in the Lamb's Book of Life will *wonder and marvel over the beast that was, and is not, and yet is.*

Verse 11 explains that the beast that was, and is not, will be the eighth king. He is the beast from the bottomless pit. This vision helps identify the eighth and last kingdom which will be formed before the Lord returns and sets up His kingdom forever.

The beast symbolizes three things:

1. The *Antichrist* is the beast that came out of the sea (many nations) *(Revelation 13)*
2. A *supernatural* being. He is the *beast out of the abyss (bottomless pit) (Revelation 11:7 & 17:8).*
3. An *empire*; the *eighth kingdom* which immediately succeeds and yet is a part of the seventh kingdom.

Revelation 17:10a

"Five are fallen"

As explained earlier these were the kingdoms of Egypt, Assyria, Babylon, Medo-Persia and Greece.

Revelation 17:10b

"One is"

The Roman Empire is the sixth kingdom which existed during John's life.

Revelation 17:10c

"The other is not yet come; and when he comes he must continue a short space."

This refers to the revived Roman Empire known today as the European Common Community. The leader of the European Common Community during the tribulation will become known as the antichrist during the last three and a half years.

Scripture states the body of the beast is *"like a leopard"* (Revelation 13:2) which is symbolic for the Kingdom of Greece *(Daniel 8, 9, 11&12)*.

In Revelation 17:12 the ten horns of the dragon have no crowns but Revelation 13 says that the ten horns of the beast have crowns.

Satan will give the ten kingdoms of the Revived Roman Empire to the antichrist to rule over them for the last three and a half years of the great tribulation.

> *"And the beast which I saw was like unto a leopard, and his feet were as the feet of a bear, and his mouth as the mouth of a lion: and the dragon gave him his power, and his seat, and great authority."*
>
> *"And there was given unto him a mouth speaking great things and blasphemies; and power was given unto him to continue forty and two months."* (Revelation 13:2&5)

[SEE ALSO: DANIEL 8:24; II THESSALONIANS 2:8-12]

The antichrist at the end of the tribulation will make kings of the leaders of the ten nations. In return the ten nations will give control of their armies to the beast.

[SEE ALSO: REVELATION 16:14]

Revelation 17:15

> *"And he said to me, "The waters which you saw, where the harlot sits, are peoples, multitudes, nations, and tongues."*

The papal church from its beginning had influence and power within the Roman Empire. This power of the papal church eventually spread to every continent, country and nation instilling its influence in every language, nationality and culture throughout the world.

Revelation 17:16

> *"And the ten horns which you saw on the beast, these will hate the harlot, make her desolate and naked, eat her flesh and burn her with fire."*

Once the antichrist has full political power and the false prophet gives all his religious authority to the antichrist, there will no longer be a need for the papal church, so the ten nation confederacy (E.C.C.) will destroy her.

Revelation 17:17

> "For God has put it into their hearts to fulfill His purpose, to be of one mind, and to give their kingdom to the beast, until the words of God are fulfilled."

God always was, is and will be in control. It is His plan that is being carried out.

Revelation 17:18

> "And the woman whom you saw is that great city which reigns over the kings of the earth."

What was a mystery to John in his day is not a mystery to us. The Roman Catholic Papal Church did not exist in John's day. When John was shown this vast world wide church claiming to be Christian but following the antichrist, he did not understand because he had nothing to reference it to.

CHAPTER 18

Revelation 18:1

> *"After these things I saw another angel coming down from heaven, having great authority, and the earth was illuminated with his glory."*

After John witnesses the destruction of Mystery Babylon, a new event unfolds before him, the destruction of the City of Babylon (Iraq/Iran/Afghanistan).

The angel is probably Michael although the Bible doesn't actually say. Michael is the defending angel of Israel in the Old Testament.

In chapter 17 Mystery Babylon was destroyed by the beast and his ten kingdoms. In this chapter the city of Babylon is destroyed by God.

In chapter 17 the kings of the earth rejoiced at the destruction of *Mystery Babylon*, but in this chapter they weep and lament because the city is destroyed.

Chapter 17 described the destruction of the religious system, whereas this chapter describes the destruction of the commercial and governmental city of Babylon where Satan has his throne.

Revelation 18:2

> *"And he cried mightily with a loud voice, saying, "Babylon the great is fallen, is fallen, and has become a habitation of*

> demons, a prison for every foul spirit, and a cage for every unclean and hated bird!"

When God destroys Babylon it will be the place where demons and evil spirits of the earth will be condemned to stay until their judgment. It will be an inescapable cage for them. The entire city and everything associated with it will be wiped out in just one hour (Revelation 18:10c).

Revelation 18:3

> "For all the nations have drunk of the wine of the wrath of her fornication, the kings of the earth have committed fornication with her, and the merchants of the earth have become rich through the abundance of her luxury."

No nation will be exempt from the pull of Babylon and the lust for material possessions and adulteries. Everything evil will be legal during the great tribulation.

[SEE ALSO: JAMES 5:1-6]

Revelation 18:4

> "And I heard another voice from heaven saying, "Come out of her, My people, lest you share in her sins, and lest you receive of her plagues."

God is calling Jews and tribulation believers to come out and separate themselves and not be partakers of the sins of Babylon so they will be free from the judgments about to fall on the city.

God did the same for Lot, Abraham's nephew when He was about to destroy Sodom and Gomorrah. God had two angels remove Lot and his family out of Sodom and Gomorrah so they would not be caught up in the destruction. *(Genesis 19:12)*

> "Leave Babylon, flee from the Babylonians! Announce this with shouts of joy and proclaim it. Send it out to the ends of the earth; say, "The LORD has redeemed His servant Jacob." (Isaiah 48:20) (NIV)

[SEE ALSO: ISAIAH 52:11; JEREMIAH 50:8; 51:6; II CORINTHIANS 6:17]

Revelation 18:5

> "For her sins have reached to heaven, and God has remembered her iniquities."

Just like the prayers of the saints reach unto heaven (Revelation 5:8&8:3&4) so the sins of the wicked reach unto heaven.

> "Arise, go to Nineveh, that great city, and cry against it; for their wickedness is come up before Me." (Jonah 1:2)

Just as God answers and blesses the prayers of the saints; so God will give the sinners their just punishment.

> "On the wicked He will rain fiery coals and burning sulfur; a scorching wind will be their lot." (Psalms 11:6) (NIV)

> "But the day Lot left Sodom, fire and sulfur rained down from heaven and destroyed them all. It will be just like this on the day the Son of Man is revealed." (Luke 17:29&30) (NIV)

[SEE ALSO: GENESIS 19:24 PROVERBS 21:15; EZEKIEL 38:22]

Revelation 18:6

> "Render to her just as she rendered to you, and repay her double according to her works; in the cup which she has mixed, mix for her double."

God doubles the punishment for Babylon because of the way she persecuted Israel through the centuries.

> "Before your eyes I will repay Babylon and all who live in Babylonia for all the wrong they have done in Zion," declares the LORD."
>
> "Babylon must fall because of Israel's slain, just as the slain in all the earth have fallen because of Babylon." (Jeremiah 51:24&49)(NIV)

[SEE ALSO: PSALMS 137:8&9; JEREMIAH 50:15&16]

Revelation 18:7&8

> "In the measure that she glorified herself and lived luxuriously, in the same measure give her torment and sorrow; for she says in her heart, 'I sit as queen, and am no widow, and will not see sorrow. Therefore her plagues will come in one day-death and mourning and famine. And she will be utterly burned with fire, for strong is the Lord God who judges her."

Babylon's pride was that she glorified herself instead of God. *(Ezekiel 28:4-10)*

   Pride was Lucifer's downfall. *(Isaiah 14:11-15)*

   Babylon said in her heart "*I sit a queen and am no widow, and will not see sorrow*"; but God has a different plan for Babylon.

[SEE ALSO: ISAIAH 47:7-11; JEREMIAH 50:34]

Revelation 18:9&10

> "And the kings of the earth who committed fornication and lived luxuriously with her will weep and lament for her, when they see the smoke of her burning, standing at a distance for fear of her torment, saying, 'Alas, alas, that great city Babylon, that mighty city! For in one hour your judgment has come.'"

When God destroys Babylon the kings of the earth will cry but none will go to help her.

Before Christ makes His triumphant return, Babylon will once again be a glorious city and the leading trade center of the world as in the days of King Nebuchadnezzar. The world will lust after her. She will be materialistically wealthy and sexually perverse, but it won't last long. Babylon will fall quick and hard.

Revelation 18:11-19

> *"And the merchants of the earth will weep and mourn over her, for no man buys their merchandise anymore: merchandise of gold and silver, precious stones and pearls, fine linen and purple, silk and scarlet, every kind of citron wood, every kind of object of ivory, every kind of object of most precious wood, bronze, iron, and marble; and cinnamon, and incense, fragrant oil and frankincense, wine and oil, fine flour and wheat, cattle and sheep, horses and chariots, and bodies and souls of men. And the fruit that your soul longed for are gone from you, and all the things which are rich and splendid have gone from you, and you shall find them no more at all. The merchants of these things, who became rich by her, will stand at a distance for fear of her torment, weeping and wailing, and saying, 'Alas, alas, that great city that was clothed in fine linen, purple, and scarlet, and adorned with gold and precious stones and pearls! 'For in one hour such great riches came to nothing.' And every shipmaster, all who travel by ship, sailors, and as many as trade on the sea, stood at a distance and cried out when they saw the smoke of her burning, saying, 'What is like this great city?' And they threw dust on their heads and cried out, weeping and wailing, and saying, 'Alas, alas, that great city, in which*

all who had ships on the sea became rich by her wealth! For in one hour she is made desolate.'"

The merchants of the earth will cry over Babylon's destruction for there will be no luxurious, materialistic items to buy or sell from her anymore. The sea captains and sailors and shipmasters will be wailing over her because their businesses and riches just went up in smoke.

[SEE ALSO: EZEKIEL 26:17-20; 27:12-25]

The almost thirty items mentioned traded out of Babylon are all luxuries, except for the last item mentioned which is terrifying. They sold the *souls of men.*

In the end times man is nothing more than another commodity to be bought and sold. All these worldly items that man lusts after shall be wiped out forever. Satan has people so blinded lusting over materialistic things of this world that they cry out *"What is like this great city!"* If they knew the scriptures they would know Babylon is a ghetto compared to the heavenly city of New Jerusalem.

Revelation 18:20

"Rejoice over her, O heaven, and you holy apostles and prophets, for God has avenged you on her!"

The people of the earth are mourning and bewailing the destruction of Babylon. But heaven is told to *"Rejoice over her destruction."* God has watched the heathen; the unsaved and the disbelievers persecute Israel, the prophets, apostles, saints and believers for almost four thousand years.

God pours His wrath out on Satan and his followers. He will destroy Satan's seat in Babylon and everyone who worshipped him. God will show no mercy. Babylon will be destroyed to ashes like Sodom and Gomorrah, never to be inhabited again.

[SEE ALSO: JEREMIAH 51:47-49]

Revelation 18:21

> "Then a mighty angel took up a stone like a great millstone and threw it into the sea, saying, "Thus with violence the great city Babylon shall be thrown down, and shall not be found anymore.""

Webster dictionary defines a millstone as "something used to crush and destroy".

Babylon will be thrown down with great violence.
[SEE ALSO: JEREMIAH 51:63&64]

So complete will the destruction of Babylon be that the phrase "Found no more at all" is repeated six times in this chapter, Babylon's destruction is forever.

Revelation 18:22

> "The sound of harpists, musicians, flutists, and trumpeters shall not be heard in you anymore. And no craftsman of any craft shall be found in you anymore. And the sound of a millstone shall not be heard in you anymore."

Babylon in the end times will be the music capital of the world. Amid the noise, hustle and bustle of its thriving economy and commercial life will be heard music from its theaters, concerts and pleasure resorts. The world's best performers will be there but that too will come to an abrupt and sudden end.

> "The gaiety of the tambourines is stilled the noise of the revelers has stopped, the joyful harp is silent." (Isaiah 24:8) (NIV)

> "And I will cause the noise of thy songs to cease; and the sound of thy harps shall be no more heard." (Ezekiel 26:13)

No craftsman shall ever be found in Babylon again, whether it is a machinist, carpenter, electrician, painter or designer - they shall no longer exist.

Revelation 18:23

> *"And the light of a lamp shall not shine in you anymore. And the voice of bridegroom and bride shall not be heard in you anymore. For your merchants were the great men of the earth, for by your sorcery all the nations were deceived."*

No light of any kind will ever shine again in Babylon. The destruction will be so great that the air will not be able to sustain even the lighting of a match.

The *"voice of bridegroom and bride shall not be heard in you anymore"* No brides or grooms will exist because Babylon will be an ash heap.

Spiritually the bridegroom (Christ) and the bride (Church) will not be found in Babylon. Since it persecuted believers the Holy Spirit cannot dwell there either.

"For by thy sorcery (witchcraft, magic, mind altering drugs, psychics and devil worship) were all nations deceived". Babylon will be so full of darkness and evil by the time of its destruction that no light, physical or spiritual will be able to penetrate.

[SEE ALSO: II KINGS 9:22B; NAHUM 3:4-6]

Revelation 18:24

> *"And in her was found the blood of prophets and saints, and of all who were slain on the earth."*

Anyone who God sent to Babylon to witness for Him was killed. Any believers or Jews who try to live in Babylon during the tribulation will be martyred.

[SEE ALSO: JEREMIAH 51:49]

CHAPTER 19

Revelation 19:1

> "After these things I heard a loud voice of a great multitude of people in heaven, saying, "Alleluia! Salvation and glory and honor and power to the Lord our God!"

After the false church and city of Babylon are destroyed John hears all the redeemed saints in heaven praising God.

Alleluia is translated as "Praise ye the Lord" in Hebrew, Aramaic and Greek.

Revelation 19:2

> "For true and righteous are His judgments, because He has judged the great harlot who corrupted the earth with her fornication; and He has avenged on her the blood of His servants shed by her."

Happy and joyous is everybody in heaven at this moment to see the false ecumenical church destroyed.

Revelation 19:3

> "Again they said, "Alleluia! And her smoke rises up forever and ever!"

They repeat Alleluia for the destruction of the city of Babylon. Her destruction is so great the smoke from it will rise up forever.

> "For it is the day of the LORD'S vengeance, the year of recompense for the cause of Zion. Its streams shall be turned into pitch, and its dust into brimstone; its land shall become burning pitch. It shall not be quenched night or day; its smoke shall ascend forever. From generation to generation it shall lie waste; no one shall pass through it forever and ever." (Isaiah 34:8-10)

Revelation 19:4

> "And the twenty-four elders and the four living creatures fell down and worshipped God who sat on the throne, saying, "Amen! Alleluia!"

The worship continues with the twenty four elders and the four living creatures on there knees before the throne praising God.

Revelation 19:5

> "Then a voice came from the throne, saying, Praise our God, all you His servants and those who fear Him, both small and great!"

Jesus commands everybody in the universe, both small and great, angels and men to praise His Father.

Revelation 19:6

> "And I heard, as it were, the voice of a great multitude, as the sound of many waters and as the sound of mighty thunderings, saying, "Alleluia! For the Lord God Omnipotent reigns!"

John hears the response to the command and he tries to put into words the magnitude, power and majesty of what he is hearing and seeing but it is impossible.

Revelation 19:7a

> "Let us be glad and rejoice and give Him glory, for the marriage of the Lamb has come,"

Babylon is destroyed. Satan is about to be cast into the bottomless pit and chained for 1,000 years. The beast and the false prophet have been cast alive into the Lake of Fire and the armies of the beast defeated. But first, just after the destruction of Babylon but before Satan's defeat at Armageddon, the marriage of the Lamb (Jesus) to His bride (the church) takes place in heaven. All who believed in Christ since His resurrection are the bride. They have been saved by grace and purged clean passing through the refiner's fire.
[SEE ALSO: MALACHI 3:3&4; I CORINTHIANS 3:11-17]

Scripture tells us the church did not exist until the day of Pentecost (Acts 2). Only those who died having surrendered their life to Jesus and understanding His finished work on the cross are the bride.

Israelites of the Old Testament, Jews of the New Testament and believers in Jesus Christ who die after the rapture are the *invited guests* to the marriage of the Lamb.
[SEE ALSO: JOHN 3:29]

John the Baptist knew that he was not part of the bride but was happy knowing that he was a friend of the bridegroom, which makes him one of the invited guests.

Revelation 19:7b&8

> "And His wife has made herself ready." "And to her it was granted to be arrayed in fine linen, clean and bright, for the fine linen is the righteous acts of the saints."

The *fine linen* is the righteousness of the saints (plural), the righteous acts and works of all the saints represent the wedding dress.

Scripture clearly shows no one is saved by works but by grace only.

[SEE ALSO: ROMANS 3:24; EPHESIANS 1:7; 2:4&5, 8&9]

So what has our works have to do with the *"bride and her fine linen dress"*? The bride does not put on her wedding dress until after she has been tried at *"the judgment seat of Christ"* where all her false works will be consumed by the purifying fire.

Our good works win for us the *"crown of life"*, the *"incorruptible crown"*, the *"crown of righteousness"* and the *"crown of glory"*.

[SEE ALSO: I CORINTHIANS 9:25; II TIMOTHY 4:8; JAMES 1:12; I PETER 5:4; REVELATION 2:10]

> *"That the genuineness of your faith, being much more precious than gold that perishes, though it is tested by fire, may be found to praise, honor, and glory at the revelation of Jesus Christ." (I Peter 1:7)*

Revelation 19:9

> *"Then He said to me, "Write: 'Blessed are those who are called to the marriage supper of the Lamb!'" And he said to me, 'These are the true sayings of God.'"*

The marriage supper is not the wedding itself. The supper is what follows after the marriage is solemnized and the bride and groom are officially husband and wife.

To be invited to this marriage feast will be quite an honor. What better place to once again break bread and drink wine with the Lord than at His wedding.

[SEE ALSO: MATTHEW 26:29; LUKE 14:15]

If Christ is the groom and the church is the bride, than who are the invited guests? The guests will consist of the Old Testament saints and Prophets such as Abel, Seth, Enoch, Noah, Abraham, Job, Moses, Esther, King David and John the Baptist. The thief on the cross is also one of the invited guests: *"I say to you, today you will be with Me in paradise." (Luke 23:43)*

The angels will be spectators and servers at the wedding feast. Angels cannot be guests because that honor is reserved for human beings only. Angels are never the recipients of the blessings of the redeemed. Scripture says of angels: *"Are they not all ministering spirits, sent forth to minister for them who shall be heirs to salvation." (Hebrews 1:14)*

The angel concludes verse 9 with: *"These are the true sayings of God."*

These are God's words and therefore they are true; Titus 1:2 and Hebrews 6:18 state *"God cannot lie"*.

Revelation 19:10

> *"And I fell at his feet to worship him. But he said to me, "See that you do not do that! I am your fellow servant, and of your brethren who have the testimony of Jesus. Worship God! For the testimony of Jesus is the spirit of prophesy."*

John is in awe of everything he witnessed. He falls at the angel's feet to worship him but the angel tells him not to because *"he is a fellow servant, and is of thy brethren (a Jew) that also have the testimony of Jesus Christ"* (a Christian). From Revelation 17:1a we see this angel was one of the seven angels that came out of the temple with the bowls. *"And there came one of the seven angels which had the seven bowls"*. This angel tells John he is not an angel of the heavenly host but one of his brethren sent by God as a messenger.
[SEE ALSO: REVELATION 22:9]

The angel tells John to *"worship God"* and no one else. *"For the testimony of Jesus is the spirit of prophesy."* When we tell people what Jesus did for us on the cross and preach the gospel we are giving Christ's testimony and His prophetic message of salvation.

Revelation 19:11a

> *"Then I saw heaven opened, and behold, a white horse. And he who sat on him was called Faithful and True."*

In the previous verses the bride and groom were preparing for the wedding. The marriage and the wedding feast takes place and is followed by the honeymoon. Usually when a Bride and Groom go on a honeymoon they take a trip someplace. This couple is no different. What more suitable place to go for a honeymoon than to the birthplace of the bride and the place where the groom purchased His wife's redemption with His own precious blood, earth.

Revelation 19:11b

> *"In righteousness He judges and makes war."*

Unlike the rider of Revelation 6:2, this rider is Jesus and has returned to judge the earth in righteousness and wage war against the wicked.

> *"But with righteousness He will judge the needy, with justice He will give decisions for the poor of the Earth. He will strike the earth with the rod of His mouth; with the breath of His lips He will slay the wicked. Righteousness will be His belt and faithfulness the sash around His waist."* (Isaiah 11:4&5)

Revelation 19:12a

> *"His eyes were like a flame of fire."*

This verse was stated in Revelation 1:14 and Revelation 2:18 also as a description of Jesus Christ our omnipotent God who sees everything. Nothing escapes His sight.

Revelation 19:12b

"On His head were many crowns."

These crowns are not ordinary crowns of earthly kings or the *"stephanous"* (Greek) *"victor's crowns"* which the 24 elders are wearing in Revelation 4:4. Christ is wearing the *"diademata"* (Greek) for the "Kingly crown" that only He is worthy to wear. The plurality of crowns point to His character as King of kings. His Diadem comprises all the diadems of the earth and of the heavenly powers.

Revelation 19:12c

"He had a name written, that no man knew, but He Himself."

When Christ returns He will have a new name, which no one has ever heard or seen before. We know it will be a *"Name above All Names"*.

[SEE ALSO: PSALMS 138:2; EPHESIANS 1:20&21]

Revelation 19:13

"He was clothed with a robe dipped in blood, and His name is called The Word of God."

The blood on Christ's robe is the enemy's blood in the day of His vengeance:

"Why is Your apparel red, and Your garments like one who treads in the winepress? I have trodden the winepress alone, and from the peoples no one was with Me. For I have trodden them in My anger, and trampled them in My fury; their blood is sprinkled upon My garments, and I have stained all My robes. For the day of vengeance is in My heart, and the year of My redeemed has come." (Isaiah 63:2-4) (NKJV)

The antichrist's domain will be in total darkness. As Christ returns, the brightness of His glory will blind the armies gathered at Armageddon. Jesus will start to speak and the bodies of the enemy will explode. Blood will spill so quickly that it will be up to the *"bridal depth of a horse"* (Approx. 4ft. deep) and approx. 177.77 miles long and wide in a very short time.

Revelation 19:14

> *"And the armies in heaven, clothed in fine linen, white and clean, followed Him on white horses."*

The armies of heaven consist of angels, Old Testament saints and Prophets, the Church and the Tribulation saints and martyrs who will accompany the Lord to fight his enemies.

[SEE ALSO: II KINGS 6:17; ISAIAH 66:15&16; ZECHARIAH 14:5C; MATTHEW 26:53; II THESSALONIANS 1:7&8; JUDE 14]

The armies follow Christ. Unlike armies of today where the high ranking officers stay in the background while the lower ranking soldiers are on the front lines, Christ is leading this charge and getting His garments bloody. It is His day of vengeance. The fine linen, white and clean symbolizes the righteousness of the group.

Revelation 19:15a

> *"Now out of His mouth goes a sharp sword, that with it He should strike the nations:"*

The sharp sword is a word picture to describe the sharpness of God's holy word and He alone will execute judgment upon the nations.

> *"For the word of God is quick, and powerful, and sharper than any two-edged sword, piercing even to the dividing asunder of soul and spirit, and of the joints and marrow,*

and is a discerner of the thoughts and intents of the heart."
(Hebrews 4:12)

To be able to discern something it must be alive, the word of God lives and breaths through the power of the Holy Spirit.

Revelation 19:15b

"He Himself will rule them with a rod of iron:"

When Christ returns to usher in the millennium and destroy the enemy, He will still have to rule those who are left with a firm but just hand.

[SEE ALSO: REVELATION 2:27; 12:5]

Revelation 19:15c

"He Himself treads the winepress of the fierceness and wrath of Almighty God."

Christ will deliver the wrath of Almighty God against the enemy. All those who refused to believe in Jesus Christ are the enemy.

Revelation 19:16

"And He has on His robe and on His thigh a name written:

'KING OF KINGS AND LORD OF LORDS'"

A warrior goes into battle with his sword on his thigh, but Christ's sword will proceed from His mouth (the word of God). On Christ's thigh His name is written *"King of kings and Lord of lords"*. His title is visible for all to see.

[SEE ALSO: DANIEL 2:47; 1 TIMOTHY 6:15; REVELATION 17:14]

Revelation 19:17&18

"Then I saw an angel standing in the sun; and he cried with a loud voice, saying to all the birds that fly in the midst of

> heaven, "Come and gather together for the supper of the great God, that you may eat the flesh of kings, the flesh of captains, the flesh of mighty men, the flesh of horses and of those who sit on them, and the flesh of all people, free and slave, both small and great."

The angel is calling all the birds of heaven to come feast on the carnage of the enemy. There is no discrimination here, they will feast on the flesh of the richest to the poorest, kings to paupers, free man to slave and any animal carnage that is there. In Ezekiel 39:17-20 God instructs the birds and the beasts to come and eat of His sacrifice.

Revelation 19:19

> "And I saw the beast, the kings of the earth, and their armies, gathered together to make war against Him who sat on the horse and against His army."

John sees the enormous army of the world called together by the antichrist to make war against Israel, but who now find themselves facing the army of the Lord.

Revelation 19:20

> "Then the beast was captured, and with him the false prophet who worked signs in his presence, by which he deceived those who received the mark of the beast and those who worshipped his image. These two were cast alive into the Lake of Fire burning with brimstone."

The beast and false prophet were not eaten by the birds which indicate a different outcome for them. They will be cast alive into the Lake of Fire forever.

Revelation 19:21

> "And the rest were killed with the sword which proceeded from the mouth of Him who sat on the horse. And all the birds were filled with their flesh."

Jesus spoke and armies died. Unlike the beast and false prophet who were cast alive into the Lake of Fire, the rest were killed and must wait for the future final judgment. As God promised when He gathered them, all the birds were filled with their flesh, yet there will be so much carnage left that it will take Israel seven months to bury all the dead.

> "And seven months shall the house of Israel be burying of them, that they may cleanse the land." (Ezekiel 39:12)

> "For wherever the carcass is, there the eagles will be gathered together." (Matthew 24:28)

CHAPTER 20

Revelation 20:1-3

> *"Then I saw an angel coming down from heaven, having the key to the bottomless pit and a great chain in his hand. He laid hold of the dragon, that serpent of old, which is the Devil and Satan, and bound him for a thousand years; and he cast him into the bottomless pit, and shut him up, and set a seal on him, so that he should deceive the nations no more till the thousand years were finished. But after these things he must be released for a little while."*

This verse does not reveal who the angel is that has the key to the bottomless pit, but Revelation 1:18 reveals who the keeper of the key is *"I am He who lives, and was dead, and behold, I am alive forevermore. Amen. And I have the keys of Hades and of Death."*

In chapter 9 when the fifth trumpet angel sounded, John *"saw an angel fall from heaven to the earth: and to him was given the key to the bottomless pit."* Jesus handed the key over to this angel who still has possession of it in this chapter. The angel opens the pit once again, chains Satan, sets a seal on him, casts him into the bottomless pit and locks it. Though scripture does not specifically give the angel's name it does give a strong indication that the angel is *Michael the Archangel* whom the Lord sent to help the angel Gabriel fight against Satan.

> "But the prince of the Persian kingdom resisted me twenty-one days. Then, Michael, one of the chief princes, came to help me, because I was detained there with the king of Persia." (Daniel 10:13)(NIV)

Jude 9 It was Michael the archangel who contended with Satan over the body of Moses "Yet Michael the archangel when contending with the devil he disputed about the body of Moses."

[SEE ALSO: REVELATION 12:7-9]

It was Michael the archangel who led God's angels in war against the dragon and his angels. This angel not only opens the bottomless pit but is powerful enough to bind Satan with a great chain. Christ doesn't bind Satan personally, but has this angel do it. If Satan were as powerful as he wants the world to believe, Jesus Christ's power and authority would have been required to accomplish this task.

> "Yet you shall be brought down to Sheol, to the lowest depths of the pit. Those who see you will gaze at you, and consider you, saying: 'Is this the man who made the earth tremble, who shook kingdoms, who made the world as a wilderness and destroyed its cities, who did not open the house of his prisoners?'" (Isaiah 14:15-17)

The place where Satan is being sent to is real. That he will be bound in chains demonstrates Satan is a being, because you cannot bind an *influence* or a *principle* of evil.

Satan is referred to as the "Prince of the Power of the Air" (Ephesians 2:2), the "god of this age" (II Corinthians 4:4) and "the ruler of the powers of darkness" (Ephesians 6:11&12) and though he has great power and influence; Satan is not omnipotent and he is not equal to Jesus Christ. Satan is an angel created by Jesus.

The binding of Satan marks the start of the millennium. People will live in peace for a thousand years with Jesus and His saints ruling and reigning on earth.

Satan is not cast into the Lake of Fire at this time, where the beast and the false prophet were thrown. God is still going to use Satan one more time after the 1,000 year millennium period is over.

The actual length of time a *"little while"* is, scripture does not say but it will show how evil man's heart truly is. As soon as Satan is loosed after 1,000 years of being bound the nations of the earth will flock back to him and desire his evil ways again. How cunning and deceiving Satan is and how hard hearted man is.

Revelation 20:4

> *"And I saw thrones, and they sat on them, and judgment was committed to them. And I saw the souls of those who had been beheaded for their witness to Jesus and for the word of God, who had not worshipped the beast or his image, and had not received his mark on their foreheads or on their hands. And they lived and reigned with Christ for a thousand years."*

John sees thrones and people sitting on the thrones handing out judgment. He also sees those who were martyred during the tribulation for the witness of Jesus. Who also live and reign with Christ for a thousand years.

There are four categories of resurrected people that have part in the *"First Resurrection"* (Revelation 20:6):

1. Christ's Church (the Bride)
2. Those who arose at the time of Christ's resurrection. Matthew 27:52&53 *"And the graves were opened; and many bodies of the saints who had fallen asleep were raised;*

and coming out of the graves after His resurrection, they went into the holy city and appeared to many."

3. The Old Testament saints and prophets
4. The tribulation saints and martyrs

The following verses show there are two totally separate resurrections.

Revelation 20:5&6a

> "But the rest of the dead did not live again until the thousand years were finished. This is the first resurrection. Blessed and holy is he who has part in the first resurrection. Over such the second death has no power."

The above verses clearly show a first resurrection to life with God the Father and Jesus and shows Christians need not fear death.

> "Knowing that He who raised up the Lord Jesus will also raise us up with Jesus, and will present us with you."
> (II Corinthians 4:14)(NKJV)

[SEE ALSO: II CORINTHIANS 5:10]

Revelation 20:11-15 clearly shows a *second resurrection* that takes place 1,000 years after the first resurrection. The second resurrection is to eternal death.

In both resurrections people are raised from the dead and reunited body and spirit. Those in the first resurrection will be enjoying eternal life in the presence of the Lord in their immortal bodies, able to think, touch, smell, taste and eat of the good things God gives us while those in the second resurrection to death will be in their immortal bodies with their sense of touch, smell, taste, thought and pain cast into eternal damnation in the Lake of Fire, suffering the flames for eternity.

> *"In hell, where he was in torment, he looked up and saw Abraham far away, with Lazarus by his side. So he called to him, 'Father Abraham, have pity on me and send Lazarus to dip the tip of his finger in water and cool my tongue, because I am in agony in this fire.' But Abraham replied, 'Son, remember that in your lifetime you received your good things, while Lazarus received bad things, but now he is comforted here and you are in agony." (Luke 16:23-25) (NIV)*

The flames will never be quenched and weeping and gnashing of teeth will go on forever and ever.

[SEE ALSO: MATTHEW 8:12; 22:13&14; LUKE 13:27&28; REVELATION 21:8]

Revelation 20:6b

> *"Be priests of God and of Christ, and shall reign with Him a thousand years."*

> *"But you are a chosen people, a royal priesthood, a holy nation, a people belonging to God, that you may declare the praises of Him who called you out of darkness into His wonderful light. Once you were not a people, but now you are the people of God; once you had not received mercy, but now you have received mercy." (I Peter 2:9&10) (NIV)*

[SEE ALSO: EXODUS 19:6A]

Some Israelites will be priests for God the Father and some Believers will be priests for Jesus.

Revelation 20:7-8a

> *"Now when the thousand years have expired, Satan will be released from his prison and will go out to deceive the nations which are in the four corners of the earth."*

When the thousand years are completed, Satan's chains will be removed and the seal that God placed on Satan will be removed.

The bottomless pit will be unlocked and Satan will be free to move about the earth once more, but just for a *"little season"* for the purpose of deceiving the nations of the earth once again.

Man just completed living 1,000 years in total peace and harmony with Jesus Christ but as soon as Satan is loosed, men will flock back to Satan and his evil deceitful ways. Satan convinces man that they can make war against Jesus and His immortal saints and angels and defeat them.

The population of the earth will flourish during the thousand year reign of Jesus. No wars, no famine, no mass destruction, no pestilence, disease or viruses because the great physician and healer will be here with us.

The government will be a "theocracy". God will rule in the person of the Lord Jesus Christ (Luke 1:32&33).

Revelation 20:8b

> *"Gog and Magog, to gather them together to battle, whose number is as the sand of the sea".*

Gog, a son of Reuben the first born of Jacob (Israel), became a prince who ruled over Meshach and Tubal (I Chronicles 5:4). Because Reuben defiled his fathers bed (Genesis 35:22) he lost his birthright to the sons of Joseph, who was a son of Jacob. According to scripture Satan will first go to Gog and Magog (modern day Russia) to deceive the people. Ezekiel 38 states Satan will than draw Persia (modern day Iran), Ethiopia (name has not changed in 3,000 years) located in southern Egypt, Libya (name has not changed since Ezekiel's time, but in the book of Genesis was known as Phut, Put, and Pul), Gomer (present day Ukraine), Togarmah (present day Armenia) and all his bands (Georgia, Yerevan, Baku, Azerbaijan, Bulgaria, Romania, Hungary, Moldavia, Yugoslavia, Albania, Istanbul, Slovenia, Croatia, Bosnia, Serbia, Herzegovina, Kosovo, Montenegro, Macedonia, Czechoslovakia) and nations from around the world into believing that they will be able to destroy the City of Jerusalem, the nation of Israel, Jesus Christ and all His saints and angels.

Revelation 20:9

> *"They went up on the breadth of the earth and surrounded the camp of the saints and the beloved city. And fire came down from God out of heaven and devoured them."*

God is so outraged at Satan and his follower's that no actual war will take place. God will send down fire from heaven and devour the enemy.

Northern Egypt, Jordan and Lebanon are not mentioned as part of the enemy that will be gathered against Israel because those lands were part of the land God promised to:

Abram *(Abraham)*

[SEE ALSO: GENESIS 15:18-21]

Isaac

[SEE ALSO: GENESIS 26:3&4]

Jacob *(Israel)*

[SEE ALSO: GENESIS 28:4&13]

Israel will already be occupying the Promised Land during the millennium.

Saudi Arabia will not fight against Israel when Satan is loosed because they are the children of Ishmael the half brother of Isaac. Abraham is their father. Hagar the bond servant is the mother of Ishmael while Sarah is the mother of Isaac. They will be living in peace from the start of the millennium.

Revelation 20:10

> "And the devil, who deceived them, was cast into the Lake of Fire and brimstone where the beast and the false prophet are. And they will be tormented day and night forever and ever."

God sends fire out of heaven and destroys all the enemies of Christ and casts Satan into the Lake of Fire where the beast and the false prophet have been burning for the last 1,000 years. Soon all the unbelievers who refused to acknowledge Jesus Christ as Lord and Savior will be joining them.

Revelation 20:11

> "Then I saw a great white throne and Him who sat on it, from whose face the earth and the heaven fled away. And there was found no place for them."

As soon as Satan is cast into the Lake of Fire, John sees the great white throne with the Father sitting on it.

[SEE ALSO: DANIEL 7:9&10]

Jesus is already on His throne in Jerusalem.

[SEE ALSO: DANIEL 7:13&14]

The judgment of the unsaved is about to begin.

So awesome is God the Father's glory that the polluted sinful earth and heaven cannot stand before God's purity. It shakes off its foundation fleeing from His presence and bursts into a ball of flame. All the impurities, sin and diseases dissolve away in the flames so that the earth is totally purified and fit to receive the presence of God Almighty.

> "Therefore I will shake the heavens, and the earth shall remove out of her place, in the wrath of the LORD of hosts, and in the day of His fierce anger." Isaiah 13:13

[SEE ALSO: ISAIAH 24:18C-20]

This is quite a contrast between the first resurrection for believers unto life *(Revelation 20:5&6)* and the second resurrection for unbelievers unto death.

Jesus, the saints, angels and all the people who stayed faithful to Christ during the millennium and after Satan was loosed for a season will be temporarily removed from the earth at the time of its fiery cleansing. As the purging is taking place the judgments of the unrighteous will also occur which includes Satan's fallen angels, the angels who left their "First Estate" *(Genesis 6:2)* and all the unbelievers.

> "Do you not know that the saints will judge the world? And if you are to judge the world, are you not competent to judge trivial cases? Do you not know that we will judge angels? How much more the things of this life!" (I Corinthians 6:2&3)

[SEE ALSO: II PETER 2:4; JUDE 6]

Revelation 20:12&13

> "And I saw the dead, small and great, standing before God, and books were opened. And another book was opened, which is the Book of Life. And the dead were judged according to their works, by the things which were written in the books. The sea gave up the dead who were in it, and Death and Hades delivered up the dead who were in them. And they were judged, each one according to his works."

Scripture doesn't specifically say which books were open but Daniel also mentioned them.

> "A fiery stream issued and came forth from before Him: thousand thousands ministered unto Him, and ten thousand times ten thousand stood before Him: the judgment was set, and the books were opened." Daniel 7:10

Which ever books they are, the words are pure, true and righteous so the wicked and the dead can be righteously judged from them.

[SEE ALSO: HOSEA 6:5]

Revelation 20:14

> "Then Death and Hades were cast into the Lake of Fire. This is the second death."

Death and Hades are the last two evils to be cast into the Lake of Fire and destroyed forever.

[SEE ALSO: ISAIAH 25:8A; I CORINTHIANS 15:54&55]

Revelation 20:15

> "And anyone not found written in the Book of Life was cast into the Lake of Fire."

There will be people judged at this time who never heard of Jesus Christ they will be judged by what they did according to their conscience.

[SEE ALSO: I CORINTHIANS 8:7; TITUS 1:15&16]

CHAPTER 21

Revelation 21:1

> "And I saw a new heaven and a new earth, for the first heaven and the first earth had passed away. Also there was no more sea."

> "For, behold, I create new heavens and a new earth: and the former shall not be remembered, nor come into mind." (Isaiah 65:17)

[SEE ALSO: II PETER 3:10-13]

The first heaven and first earth were created before time as we know it. They were created in eternity in the timeless past.

> "In the beginning God created the heaven and the earth." (Genesis 1:1)

> "I beheld the earth, and indeed it was without form, and void; and the heavens they had no light." (Jeremiah 4:23)

What caused the earth to become a waste after its original creation is not specified but scripture informs us that *Lucifer* before he became the fallen angel we know as Satan was given charge to take care of this earth (Ezekiel 28:12-17).

There is no conflict between God and scientists when you look at the scriptures in an unbiased manner concerning how long the earth has been here. Starting with Genesis 1:1, the earth could be billions, or trillions of years old but man has only been here 6,000 years (Genesis 1:26-28 &31).

When the time came in God's purpose to restore the earth to a habitable state for the human race, He did it in six days of 24 hour lengths and the seventh 24 hour day He rested. We call this the *creation week* (Genesis 1:3-31& 2:1-3).

When Jesus Christ returns to the earth to start the millennial kingdom the Mount of Olives will be divided in two and the mountains and valleys of Palestine and the world will be leveled. The Dead Sea will become fresh water and teaming with life and the Middle East as well as the rest of the world will be changed *(Ezekiel 47:6-12; Zechariah 14:4, 8&9)*. The climatic and physical changes of the earth will reverse back to what they were before the time of Noah's flood. Man will once again live over 900 years.

At the great white throne judgment the earth and the heaven surrounding it will be renovated by fire. The exterior surface shall be completely changed by the fire as will the atmosphere we live in. All sin, disease, germs, thorns, thistle, weeds, pests, insects, sickness, etc. will be destroyed and the air we breathe will be 100% pure. God will provide a safe haven for those of the earth during the cleansing of the earth by fire. Once the earth is totally cleansed, He will place the people back on the earth to replenish it. God is not limited to what He can or can not do, or how He does it.

The foundation of the earth was not destroyed in Genesis 1:2 or Genesis 7:11-24 by water and the foundation of the earth will not be destroyed by fire. The earth will be purified, cleansed and the surface changed by the extreme heat. The intensity of the fire will cause the oceans to evaporate and dry up: *"and there was no more sea." (Revelation 21: 1b)*

Revelation 21:2

> *"Then I, John, saw the holy city, New Jerusalem, coming down out of heaven from God, prepared as a bride adorned for her husband."*

The old Jerusalem will be destroyed in the fire that cleanses the earth because it too is polluted and corrupt with sin. From this wording, John does not see an actual building, but the *people* make up the New Jerusalem prepared to look like a bride adorned for her husband. These people are all those whose names have been found written in the Book of Life since man was created including those whose names were found in the Book of Life at the White Throne Judgment. Heaven and earth has now been cleansed and 100% restored to its perfect state. All tears are wiped away as is all memory of the old sinful heaven and earth.

Revelation 21:3

> *"And I heard a loud voice from heaven saying, "Behold, the tabernacle of God is with men, and He will dwell with them, and they shall be His people, and God Himself will be with them and be their God."*

This great voice John hears might be one of the archangels who help guard the throne of God. Whoever it is, two important things are revealed.

1. Man will still exist, but now it will be in a sinless state as Adam and Eve were before their fall.
2. God *is* the tabernacle and will dwell with the whole house of Israel now in their Promised Land.

[SEE ALSO: EZEKIEL 43:7]

Revelation 21:4

> *"And God will wipe away every tear from their eyes; there shall be no more death, nor sorrow, nor crying; and there shall be no more pain, for the former things have passed away."*

Death, pain, suffering and disease are totally destroyed when the White Throne Judgment is completed. It will be a "Perfect Kingdom" when God Himself will dwell with us on the earth.

Revelation 21:5

> "Then He who sat on the throne said, "Behold, I make all things new." And He said to me, "Write: for these words are true and faithful.""

> "Therefore, if anyone is in Christ, he is a new creation; old things have passed away; behold, all things have become new." (II Corinthians 5:17)

God tells John: "write, for these words are true and faithful." These are the same words the angel said of God in (John 14:6, 23&24; Revelation 19:9b). God is truth and so are His words.

Revelation 21:6-8

> "And He said to me, "It is done! I am the Alpha and the Omega, the Beginning and the End. I will give of the fountain of the water of life freely to him who thirsts. He who overcomes shall inherit all things, and I will be his God and he shall be My son. But the cowardly, unbelieving, abominable, murderers, sexually immoral, sorcerers, idolaters, and all liars shall have their part in the lake which burns with fire and brimstone, which is the second death."

This is like a brief synopsis of the entire book of Revelation. Jesus confirms once again:

1. He is "Alpha and Omega, Beginning and the End".
2. Everlasting life with a Father and son relationship just like Jesus has with His Father.
3. He will be our God and we will be His son.

[SEE ALSO: HEBREWS 8:10]

4. Those who reject the invitation to accept Jesus as their Lord and Savior will be cast into the Lake of Fire for all eternity.

God makes a new covenant with Israel, all sin is wiped away and Israel returns to God.

Revelation 21:9

> *"Then one of the seven angels who had the seven bowls filled with the seven last plagues, came to me and talked with me, saying, "Come, I will show you the bride, the Lamb's wife."*

God is now on earth ruling and reigning with Jesus. Israel has inherited their promised land. One of the angels who poured out one of the seven last plagues comes over to John and says he will show John the bride, the Lamb's wife. The church becomes Christ's wife after the rapture but before Christ's return to earth; so the church is now the Lamb's wife. John is about to see the bride in all her splendor and glory.

Revelation 21:10&11

> *"And he carried me away in the Spirit to a great and high mountain, and showed me the great city, the holy Jerusalem, descending out of heaven from God, having the glory of God. And her light was like a most precious stone, like a jasper stone, clear as crystal."*

This is the new earth, the oceans and seas are gone. John is taken by the angel to the top of a very great high mountain to witness the new perfect Jerusalem coming down from heaven to the earth. It has the glory of God shining through out. John describes it the best way he knows how.

Jasper is gold in appearance but like clear glass in substance. It is a crystal which has a golden hue to it. This is the same stone John used to describe the brilliance of God the Father and Jesus sitting on the throne *(Revelation 4:3a)*. God's perfect city is coming down from heaven; Christ's wife, perfect in beauty and splendor. This verifies the scriptures which say that we will be like Him (Christ) and will be "children of God".

Revelation 21:12-14

> *"Also she had a great and high wall with twelve gates, and twelve angels at the gates, and names written on them, which are the names of the twelve tribes of the children of Israel: three gates on the east, three gates on the north, three gates on the south, and three gates on the west. Now the wall of the city had twelve foundations, and on them were the names of the twelve apostles of the Lamb."*

Christ built His church using the apostles as the foundation, with Himself as the Chief Cornerstone. The apostles went throughout the world spreading the gospel and building Christ's church.
[SEE ALSO: EPHESIANS 2:19-22]

The gates of the New Jerusalem are set up the same way the camp of Israel was set up when they wandered through the desert for forty years.

Revelation 21:15

> *"And he who talked with me had a golden reed to measure the city, its gates, and its wall."*

The angel hands John a reed. A reed is equal to ten and a half feet.
[SEE ALSO: REVELATION 11:1&2A]

Revelation 21:16

> *"And the city is laid out as a square and its length is as great as its breadth. And he measured the city with the reed:*

> *twelve thousand furlongs. Its length, breadth and height are equal."*

John measures the city to be: twelve thousand furlongs (a furlong equals 1/9 of a mile). The New Jerusalem will be 1,333.33 miles in length, 1,333.33 miles in width, and 1,333.33 miles high. The angel mentions that the city is laid out as a *square*, not a *cube*; but the height is the same distance as the length and width which reveals that the city is *pyramid* shaped.

Revelation 21:17

> *"Then he measured its wall: one hundred and forty-four cubits, according to the measure of a man, that is, of the angel."*

One Cubit equals 18 inches, this makes the wall 216 feet thick.

Revelation 21:18

> *"And the construction of its wall was of jasper; and the city was pure gold, like clear glass."*

The city is 100% pure gold, flawless, so it reflects like crystal. Imagine what this will look like? 1,333.33 miles square and high of pure gold shining off the brilliance of God's glory, but it doesn't stop there, it gets even better.

Revelation 21:19&20

> *"And the foundations of the wall of the city were adorned with all kinds of precious stones: the first foundation was jasper; the second sapphire, the third chalcedony, the fourth emerald, the fifth sardonyx, the sixth sardius, the seventh chrysolite, the eighth beryl, the ninth topaz, the tenth chrysoprase, the eleventh jacinth, and the twelfth amethyst."*

The foundation walls are decorated with magnificent precious stones: "jasper" we already discussed. "Sapphire" is similar to a diamond in hardness but is blue in color. "Chalcedony" can be either a sky blue agate stone or a fine grained multicolored stone that comes with the various colors arranged in stripes, blended in cloud like or moss like forms. An "emerald" is a bright green color. "Sardonyx" is a red and white stone. "Sardius" is a common jewel found in both a red or honey color. The sardius is used with jasper in describing the glory of God in Revelation 4:3. "Chrysolyte" is a transparent stone that can be either gold or pale green in color. "Beryl" is a sea green color. "Topaz" is yellow-green in color and is transparent. "Chrysoprasus" is an apple-green color. "Jacinth" is violet in color and "amethyst" is purple in color.

The sparkle of the Holy City will be seen throughout the universe.

Revelation 21:21

> "And the twelve gates were twelve pearls: each individual gate was of one pearl. And the street of the city was pure gold, like transparent glass."

Imagine the size of those pearls. The street is 100% pure gold and transparent. The word street is singular, which gives all the more reason to believe that the city is *pyramid* in shape.

Revelation 21:22

> "But I saw no temple in it, for the Lord God Almighty and the Lamb are its temple."

This verse gives insight that unlike the previous temples built by man; John says he *"saw no temple (building) in it (New Jerusalem): for the Lord God Almighty and the Lamb are the temple"* (a living temple; not a material temple).

In the days of Moses God established the tabernacle where He would come to be in the midst of the people in what is known as the "Holy of Holies".

While Solomon (King David's son) was king, he built a temple following God's blueprints. The temple was eventually destroyed due to the disobedience of Israel. Many years later, the temple was rebuilt, but not up to the standard of Solomon's temple.

After Christ ascended into heaven He sent the Holy Spirit to live within the bodies of the believers to teach, guide and comfort us.

[SEE ALSO: I CORINTHIANS 6:19&20; II CORINTHIANS 6:16A]

In the Perfect Kingdom God Almighty will be here on earth making no need for a material temple. The entire city of Jerusalem will be the glorious temple.

[SEE ALSO: HEBREWS 12:22]

Revelation 21:23

> *"And the city had no need of the sun or of the moon to shine in it, for the glory of God illuminated it, and the Lamb is its light."*

> *"The sun will no more be your light by day, nor will the brightness of the moon shine on you, for the LORD will be your everlasting light, and your God will be your glory. Your sun will never set again, and your moon will wane no more; the LORD will be your everlasting light, and your days of sorrow will end. Then will all your people be righteous and they will possess the land forever. They are the shoot I have planted, the work of My hands, for the display of My splendor. The least of you will become a thousand, the smallest a mighty nation. I am the LORD; in its time I will do this swiftly." (Isaiah 60:19-22) (NIV)*

The Lord is not saying there will be no more sun and moon. He is saying there will be no need of them within New Jerusalem because the glory of God will illuminate it. The rest of the earth outside of the holy city will still need the light of the sun and the moon, to help keep the order of things.

Revelation 21:24

> "And the nations of those who are saved shall walk in its light, and the kings of the earth bring their glory and honor into it."

There will be no more sin or evil in the world, but there will still be human life on this earth. The saved nations are those that sided with Israel. The saved nations do not dwell within the walls of the city of the New Jerusalem, because that is reserved for the bride of Christ, the Old and New Testament saints, prophets, martyrs, angels and Israel. The kings that God will appoint to rule the saved nations will come to pay honor and glory to the Lord God in New Jerusalem.

Once the eternal future begins, ethnic/racial differences no longer exist. God's promise to Israel is that the descendants of Abraham, Isaac and Jacob shall inherit this earth for a *"thousand generations"*.

[SEE ALSO: DEUTERONOMY 7:9; I CHRONICLES 16:15; PSALMS 105:8]

God could not fulfill this promise to the people of Israel unless He keeps them on this earth. God promised *"For as the new heavens and the new earth, which I will make, will remain before Me, says the LORD, so will your (Israel) seed and your (Israel) name remain." (Isaiah 66:22)*

When this earth is cleansed by fire, the people of the saved nations will also be judged and cleansed by God and have no sin; therefore they can no longer pass sin on to the next generations.

Revelation 21:25

"Its gates shall not be shut at all by day (there shall be no night there)."

There is complete safety. Sin no longer exists so there is no need to shut the gates. The glory of God will be in the city, God all in all; Father, Son and Holy Spirit. There will be no night within the city.

Revelation 21:26

"And they shall bring the glory and the honor of the nations into it."

The nations will be able to come and worship God no matter what time of the day or night it is, for within the walls of the city there is no night.

Revelation 21:27

"But there shall by no means enter it anything that defiles, or causes an abomination or a lie, but only those who are written in the Lamb's Book of Life."

This verse reiterates the seriousness of not knowing Jesus Christ as your Lord and Savior. Everyone who does not believe in Jesus and is not found in the Book of Life is now burning in the Lake of Fire. Any other sin, pestilence, disease or evil that was left in the world was burnt up when the earth was purified by fire.

CHAPTER 22

Revelation 22:1

> *"And he showed me a pure river of water of life, clear as crystal, proceeding from the throne of God and of the Lamb."*

Think of the purest, cleanest water that you have ever seen or tasted and it will be like the dirtiest, most polluted water you have ever seen when compared to the water from the River of Life. The life giving water will flow out from beneath the very throne of God.

> *"You give them drink from Your River of Delights. For with You is the fountain of life; in Your light we see light." Psalms 36:8b&9 (NIV)*

The living water echoes the promise of Jesus to the woman at the well *(John 4:10-14)*.

Revelation 22:2

> *"In the middle of its street, and on either side of the river, was the tree of life, which bore twelve fruits, each tree yielding its fruit every month. And the leaves of the tree were for the healing of the nations."*

The golden street in New Jerusalem will be lined with the Tree of Life running through the center. On each side of the river of living waters the Tree of Life will be growing. The Tree of Life will grow twelve different types of fruit. A different fruit *every month*, which reveals time, still exists for those outside the city walls who are still guided by the sun, moon and stars to tell days and seasons. The leaves of the trees are for the healing of the nations; not that there is any sickness, sin, or disease, but to preserve them in health, just as Adam and Eve would have been preserved in eternal health if they had not sinned by disobeying God and eating of the tree of knowledge of good and evil in the Garden of Eden.

[SEE ALSO: GENESIS 2:16&17]

Revelation 22:3a

"And there shall be no more curse."

Jerusalem will never be attacked again. The inhabitants of Jerusalem will live in peace forevermore. The curse of Adam will be removed. The curse for the ground will be removed, no more laboring among thorns and thistle.

[SEE ALSO: ZECHARIAH 14:11]

Revelation 22:3b

"But the throne of God and of the Lamb shall be in it, and His servants shall serve Him."

There will be no man made temple to serve in, for God Himself is the temple. The servants will be serving the Father and Jesus personally. What an honor.

Revelation 22:4a

"They shall see His face."

All throughout scripture it states no one can see God or look upon Him *"lest they die"* because of sin.

[SEE ALSO: EXODUS 33:20; I TIMOTHY 6:16; I JOHN 4:12]

The angel tells John because sin no longer exists we will be able to look directly into the face of God without fear, shame or guilt just as Adam did before he sinned. *(Genesis 3:8)*

"Blessed are the pure in heart: for they shall see God." (Matthew 5:8)

"For now we see through a glass darkly; but then face to face." (I Corinthians 13:12)

Rev. 22:4b

"And His name shall be in their foreheads."

How awesome to be able to have God's name on our foreheads for the entire universe to see.

"Nevertheless, God's solid foundation stands firm, sealed with this inscription: "The Lord knows those who are His." (II Timothy 2:19a)

Revelation 22:5

"And there shall be no night there: They need no lamp nor light of the sun, for the Lord God gives them light. And they shall reign forever and ever."

This verse reiterates Revelation 21:23-25. How comforting to know we will never worry about being in the dark again. The light will be constant, never dimming or fading. We will not worry about warmth from the sun or heating from a furnace. God will be our constant light and warmth; the perfect temperature, never too hot or too cold as we reign with Him forever.

Revelation 22:6

"Then he said to me, "These words are faithful and true." And the Lord God of the holy prophets sent His angel to show His servants the things which must shortly take place."

These are the same words of confirmation used in Revelation 21:5. This is an interesting statement the angel makes for he is talking plural - *"show His servants"*. The angel was sent by God not just to give this message to John but to all who believe, to be witnesses to the world that what is written in this book is true and will soon take place. He will come quickly and take vengeance upon all those that rejected Him.

Revelation 22:7

"Behold, I am coming quickly! Blessed is he who keeps the words of the prophecy of this book."

At the very beginning the Lord gave a blessing to those who read, hear and keep the sayings of this book. Now, at the ending of this book the Lord is giving another blessing to those who believe what they have read. This book can be frightening to those who have not studied scripture and do not realize the terrifying things written in this book are for those who do not believe in Jesus Christ.

For believers, we have a marvelous kingdom and our very own mansions waiting for us. We will walk on a street paved of gold and the river of living water flowing through the center of the city with the Tree of Life lining each side of the river. We will be in the presence of Almighty God forever.

God says He will add extra blessings to those who read and believe the prophecies of this book. He already gives us wonderful blessings each and every day of our lives. Many we never see because we are caught up in our busy day to day activities and forget to give God His daily praise worship and honor that He so richly deserves. He loves us despite all our shortcomings because He created us and more importantly because we believe in His only begotten Son, Jesus Christ.

Revelation 22:8&9

> "Now I, John, saw and heard these things. And when I heard and saw, I fell down to worship before the feet of the angel which showed me these things. Then he said to me, "See that you do not do that for I am your fellow servant, and of your brethren the prophets and of those who keep the words of this book. Worship God"

John is so overwhelmed by everything he has seen and heard that he forgets and once again falls down at the angel's feet to worship him. As in Revelation 19:10, the angel tells John not to worship him. This angel (messenger) was once one of the Old Testament prophets, who were given the honor and privilege along with six others to pour out the last seven bowls, filled with the wrath of God upon the earth.

The Bible consistently tells us to worship God and God only. No other man, angel, statue, icon or idol of any kind is to ever be worshipped above God.

[SEE ALSO: EXODUS 20:2-5A; MATTHEW 4:10B; LUKE 4:8B]

Even the most powerful of the angels: Michael and Gabriel refused the worship of man. The only reason Jesus Christ would have for accepting the worship of man is because He truly is the Son of the Living God.

Revelation 22:10

> "And he said to me, "Do not seal the words of this book, for the time is at hand."

Daniel was told to shut the book because it was for far in the future (*Daniel 8:26; 12:4, 9*). Daniel wrote the words through the inspiration of the Holy Spirit. Daniel had no idea what the words which he wrote meant, but this is a great example of how even though the apostles and prophets wrote the words down in their own handwriting, it was God's words they were writing, not their own.

In these end times which we are living in it is now possible to see how the Book of Daniel, the Book of Revelation and the Old and New Testament work in unison to help give us a clear picture and understanding of what is to happen to believers and unbelievers alike in these last days and in eternity.

If two thousand years ago the angel warned John *"The time is at hand"*, how much closer are we today to Christ's return?

Out of billions, maybe even trillions of books ever written from the beginning of mankind 6,000 years ago, only the Scriptures have ever contained writings of events which will happen, sometimes thousands of years ahead of time, in the exact way they will happen. It tells of the birth of a single person, by name, how He will be born, where He will be born, who will bear Him, what His life will entail, why He was born, how He will die, that He will rise from the dead and why He will rise from the dead. Still people harden their hearts and refuse to believe the truth.

Revelation 22:11

> *"He who is unjust, let him be unjust still; he who is filthy, let him be filthy still; he who is righteous, let him be righteous still; he who is holy, let him be holy still."*

The angel is revealing to John no one is getting into heaven by any other means except through Jesus Christ. If the unjust is unjust let him stay that way so when he stands before God at the White Throne Judgment he will not be able to try to talk his way into heaven. The same holds true for the filthy and anybody else who refuses to believe in Jesus. There will be no rest for the wicked.

[SEE ALSO: PSALMS 95:11; HEBREWS 3:11&12]

But he that is righteous and holy and believes in Jesus let them continue on that path so they can stand before God and hear Him say: *"Well done, good and faithful servant; you have been faithful over a few things, I will make you ruler over many things: enter into the joy of your Lord." (Matthew 25:23)*
[SEE ALSO: ISAIAH 57:1&2]

Revelation 22:12

"And behold, I am coming quickly, and My reward is with Me, to give to every one according to his work."

Jesus is telling us He is just. He uses the same warning at the end of this book that he used at the beginning of this book *"Behold, I come quickly"* which is also translated as *"Behold, I come suddenly" (Revelation 3:3).*

The word reward is singular; the reward is heaven or hell because you either believe in Jesus Christ or you don't.

Revelation 22:13

"I AM THE ALPHA AND THE OMEGA, THE BEGINNING AND THE END, THE FIRST AND THE LAST."

Christ is making this declaration. Jesus always was and always will be. Before Him there was nothing *(John 1:1-3)*, and after Him there is nothing *(Isaiah 44:6)*.

Revelation 22:14

"Blessed are those who do His commandments that they may have the right to the tree of life, and may enter through the gates into the city."

The people from the nations dwelling outside New Jerusalem will have the right to eat of the Tree of Life and enter into the city of the New Jerusalem where God, the saints and the angels dwell.

Revelation 22:15

> "But outside are dogs and sorcerers and sexually immoral and murderers and idolaters, and whoever loves and practices a lie."

This verse is a flash back to the 1,000 year millennium period. It almost seems out of place here. There will still be evil and sinners during the millennium though Christ will be here in person ruling and reigning with His saints. Once the thousand years are over, these evil doers will be destroyed and cast into the Lake of Fire.

Revelation 22:16a

> "I, Jesus, have sent My angel to testify to you these things in the churches."

Jesus verifies He is the one who sent the angel to testify all these things as a warning to the churches.

Revelation 22:16b

> "I am the Root and the Offspring of David."

Jesus comes from the royal lineage of King David.
[SEE ALSO: ISAIAH 11:1; JEREMIAH 23:5&6]

Revelation 22:16c

> "The Bright and Morning Star"

Jesus lights our way day or night.

> "We also have the prophetic word made more sure, which you do well to heed as a light that shines in a dark place, until the day dawns and the morning star rises in your hearts." (II Peter 1:19)

[SEE ALSO: REVELATION 2:28]

Revelation 22:17

> "And the Spirit and the bride say, "Come!" And let him who hears say, "Come!" And let him who thirsts come. And whoever desires, let him take the water of life freely."

John is making his closing statement. Notice it is the Holy Spirit and the believers who are calling others to come to Jesus. All those that are thirsty for the word of God are invited to come. All those who heed the call to come are invited to drink of the water of life.

Revelation 22:18

> "For I testify to everyone who hears the words of the prophecy of this book: If anyone adds to these things, God will add to him the plagues that are written in this book."

This is a stern and devastating warning John issues here. The Mormons should take heed of this warning for they have added to the scriptures by saying some other angel not named in the scriptures came and gave them another book to add on to God's word. These verses are clear there are no other books or verses to the scriptures after Revelation.

[SEE ALSO: DEUTERONOMY 4:2; 12:32; PROVERBS 30:5&6]

These people are in danger of having the plagues of Revelation and Exodus come upon them. Woe unto them and any other religions or individuals adding to or taking away from the word of God.

Revelation 22:19

> "If any man takes away from the words of the book of this prophecy, God shall take away his part out of the book of life."

This warning is to anyone who purposely changes the word of God, its meaning or who ridicule, scoff, detract from, say unreal things and/or purposely reword the Holy Scriptures to what they think it should say or mean.

> "All scripture is given by inspiration of God, and is profitable for doctrine, for reproof, for correction, for instruction in righteousness." (II Timothy 3:16)

[SEE ALSO: REVELATION 20:15]

Revelation 22:20

> "He who testifies to these things says, "Surely I am coming quickly." Amen. Even so, come, Lord Jesus!"

It is Jesus who is testifying these words are true. John is just writing them down.

Jesus says "He comes quickly" (suddenly).

John says "Amen". Even so, come, Lord Jesus (maranatha).

Revelation 22:21

> "The grace of our Lord Jesus Christ be with you all. Amen."

John closes the writing of this book with a blessing.

My prayer is when the time comes that I am standing face to face with the Lord, He will say to me: "Well done, you good and faithful servant: you have been faithful over a few things, I will make you ruler over many things: Enter into the joy of your Lord" (Matthew 25:21).

Maranatha!

About the Author

I was born on the east side of Buffalo, New York on December 3rd, 1949.

I served four years in the Air Force from 1968 through 1972 and four years in the Air Force Reserves from 1981 through 1985

It was in a small east side of Buffalo machine shop where my entire life changed through asking Jesus Christ to be my Lord and Savior.

The Holy Spirit lit a fire within me on that 15th day of October 1980 which is still burning strong today. God instilled in my heart an unquenchable drive for studying the end times and end time scriptural prophecy.

In the mid-90's while teaching the book of Revelation to a small group, the Lord inspired me to write about this book to help others understand what is probably considered the most difficult, mysterious and misunderstood book of the Bible. My hope is many will come to a saving relationship with Jesus Christ as a result.

Having been a fire fighter for more than 30 years, I know what it is like to walk in flames, heat and choking black smoke. I have agonizingly witnessed charred bodies carried from disaster sites. I believe this is a minute glimpse of what hell must be like.

As you read this book, I pray you will understand you need not be destined to an eternity of suffering. There is peace, joy and security to be had through knowing Jesus Christ as your personal

Lord and Savior. He is the one constant, absolute truth in life. He is there twenty-four hours a day, seven days a week. He never takes a break; He never sleeps and He is there for you if you believe in Him.

I believe the book of Revelation is the most joyful and glorious book of the scriptures for a believer in Jesus Christ. Satan does not want you to know that nor does he want you to know he was already defeated at the cross of Christ.

I hope you will enjoy reading this book as much as I enjoyed writing it, and I hope through reading this book God will open up your heart and mind to know Him better.

I have tried to write this book as simple to read and understand as possible. The explanation for all the "signs" and "symbols" found in the book of Revelation are revealed throughout the Scriptures.

This book is scriptural and factual to the best of my knowledge and ability. I have indicated my personal opinion as such where it is given.

Frank Biela

www.ingramcontent.com/pod-product-compliance
Lightning Source LLC
LaVergne TN
LVHW020926090426
835512LV00020B/3225